Perseverance

God bless,

Richard

4/10/2019

Perseverance

Journey of a Child Warrior

Richard Willett

First Edition: November 2016

Edited by Raven Dodd, Preserving the Author's Voice
www.ravendodd.com

ISBN 1539803228
ISBN 13: 9781539803225
Library of Congress Control Number: 2016918274
CreateSpace Independent Publishing Platform
North Charleston, South Carolina

Dedication

For Mom, Dad, and my little sister Donna.

Acknowledgements

~♪

To my wife Cheryl, for a lifetime of having the confidence that I could.

To my best friend Bob Sands, my cousin Fred Bryant, and to my entire family who always saw me as I am.

To my editor Raven Dodd, Preserving the Author's Voice, for her skills in making this a story you will enjoy reading and for successfully coaching me through the arduous experience of writing.

To Trish Leonard, TLC Marketing & Creative Services, Inc., for creating a book cover that professionally represents the story inside. The cover is that most important first impression I desired.

To Dr. Robert D. Klausner, MD, FACS, for reviewing the medical terms and practices of the period and his staff for their support and encouragement.

Introduction

As a child, I experienced an illness that presented me with many challenges while growing up and throughout my adult life. Over the years, the challenges I faced never decreased, they just changed. At some point, I felt compelled to write this story. Interestingly, I found myself writing and writing until I realized I had written so much, I had too much for one book. I wasn't sure what to do, but I finally came to the conclusion that if I were going to finish the story, I would be writing a series of books. There is a conclusion to this story that makes it all worthwhile and in many ways I wish I could just tell you the beginning and the end, but the end wouldn't be nearly as meaningful if you didn't read the entire story.

I've been reluctant to take responsibility for successfully living this life because frequently people give me too much credit for living through the challenges I've faced. I have many friends and relatives who have successfully faced challenges that I have not and would never want to face, and too often they're not recognized. I am a humble man and I'm grateful for having the strength to endure through my weaknesses, but that I credit to God.

I purposely didn't place the first book in the town and city where the action took place. I refer to them as the Town and the City. Note the capital T and C. I did it because this isn't my story, it's our story. I want you to recognize yourself in the pages of this book and those to follow. I also prefer to capitalize Mom and Dad whenever I refer to my parents directly or indirectly. They both were totally unprepared for the challenges and heartache they faced, but they endured and provided me with an example to follow. They deserve the caps but more importantly the recognition of their wisdom. I phonetically spelled some words in the book because I have a regional accent that I wanted to include. It's not overwhelming, but I do have some odd pronunciations. My editor adds that I also make some odd grammatical choices, but she was willing to allow me to write as I speak, so these are intentional. The names of some of the characters in this narrative have been changed to protect their privacy.

My hope is that this story will enrich your life in some way. Enjoy the read!

> *Consider it pure joy, my brothers and sisters, whenever you face trials of many kinds, because you know that the testing of your faith produces perseverance. Let perseverance finish its work so that you may be mature and complete, not lacking anything.* James 1:2-4 NIV

CHAPTER 1

The Beginning

～⁊

It's Dad's first day back to work after vacation and he's in a panic as he rushes down the stairs and out of the apartment. He yells back to Mom as he leaves, "Call me when you know. I'll tell Jean you need to use the phone."

I've never seen Dad in such a state. One moment we're in Mom and Dad's bedroom, I'm lying on the floor in pain and then Dad's dressed and running out the door. I hurt so much all over. Mom gently picks me up; I can see tears streaming down her cheeks. This has to be a problem—a big one. I've never seen Mom cry.

"Henri?" It's Jean calling from downstairs.

"I'm coming, Jean. I'll … I'll be right down." Mom stops for a moment looking around the room; she seems confused. Finally, Mom turns toward the door, quickly walks out of the room and down the stairs. She lays me on the couch and runs out the door without saying a word. Jean looks as bad as Mom; she's holding Bobby like somebody's going to take him away.

Jean keeps saying everything's going to be okay, but she doesn't act it. She's biting her bottom lip and looking outside for Mom. Her face is red and contorted like she's ready to burst into tears. What's so terrible?

Mom's coming back in the door. She tells Jean the doctor's coming.

Jean starts out the door and turns to Mom. "I hope it's not …" She doesn't finish the sentence. Jean and Bobby are gone as fast as they came. Mom sits in the chair, rocking with her hand to her mouth. I can see she's shaking. She seems to be holding back a scream.

She picks me up and holds me tight. I can feel her heart pounding against my chest. I guess we're waiting for the doctor. The pain is getting worse and Mom looks like she's going to collapse any minute.

It seems like forever, but finally there's a knock at the door. Mom lays me on the couch and runs to the door. It's the doctor.

"How's he doing?"

"No better. He just falls—he can't stand and he keeps saying he hurts."

The doctor touches Mom's shoulder and says, "It's okay. I'll check him."

The doctor takes just a few minutes to examine me, slowly shakes his head and walks to the window. He's just staring out the window. Mom's waiting for him to say something, but he's just staring. What's he looking at? It's a dreary day; there's nothing to look at but rain. Mom's still waiting. He's got the same expression I saw on Jean's face.

Yesterday started out great. We went to Aunt Leota and Uncle Windy's for lunch. I was playing with my cousins Fred and Little Leota, but I began to feel sick, so we went home. When we got home, Jean and Bobby came over. Mom told Jean I was running a fever, so they didn't stay, but before they left, Mom and Jean got into an argument with Dad. He wanted to call the doctor, but Jean and Mom said no, I was teething.

Mom was uncomfortable with the idear of calling the doctor. She's still recovering from her last visit to the doctor a few weeks ago. She'd been worried that I didn't have any tears when I cried. Mom thought it was abnormal. The doctor told her it was normal, to relax and not panic with every little sniffle. Dad was mad that Mom didn't want to call the doctor. He told Mom that if anything happened to me, he would never forgive her.

Last night was a fitful night for the three of us. My stomach hurt and I couldn't sleep. Mom and Dad had me in their bed; none of us slept. At some point I must have fallen asleep because I woke up in my bed. When Dad came to check on me, he picked me up and brought me back to their room. He set me on the floor to walk to Mom and I collapsed. He tried a second time and my legs buckled under me again.

Mom's staring at the doctor. Finally, I hear Mom say, "Does he have polio?"

The doctor slowly looks down at the floor and says softly, "I think so."

What's polio? Is that why I hurt and can't stand?

The doctor suddenly says: "Call your husband. Take Ricky to emergency at Our Lady. Where's your phone? I need to call the hospital."

Mom tells the doctor he'll have to go next door to use Jean's phone. He says he'll call Dad too. Mom gives the doctor the phone number where Dad works and he leaves. Mom and I are alone again. There's a feeling of helplessness in the apartment.

The apartment is in a low income apartment complex. It's a small complex made up of long two story buildings with four apartments in each building. The apartments are small: a kitchen and living room on the first floor and two bedrooms and a bath on the second.

Mom and Dad lived with relatives after they were married and we moved into this apartment about a year ago. It's a federal housing project for veterans that Mom and Dad had been waiting anxiously to be built. Everyone calls it "the Project."

The Project is in a small Town across the river from the City. The tenants are young families just starting their lives. Here there's hope for a better life and for Mom and Dad things had just started looking up. Dad's an automotive machinist trainee at an auto parts store. He also works nights pumping gas and in the summer he picks asparagus at a farm nearby.

It's just been a few years since Dad returned from Japan as part of the army occupation force after the war. Mom and Dad dated before he left, and against my grandparents' wishes, planned on getting married when he returned. They didn't think Dad would amount to much. He grew up in the poorest part of the Town in a rundown row house. Mom grew up in a bordering town, Westside, on a nice street in a single family home. Both families are large and didn't have much, but Dad definitely had less.

On a Wednesday morning in August, shortly after Dad returned from Japan, he drove to Nana and Papa's house in a borrowed car. With little planning and no blessings, Mom walked out of the house and got in the car. They drove to the justice of the peace and got married. Dad's still borrowing cars. He uses the company truck nights and weekends.

Mom says they started out broke. I guess we still are. They couldn't afford a honeymoon, and there weren't any apartments they could afford, so they moved in with Aunt Ruth and Uncle Al. Aunt Ruth is one of Dad's older sisters. Dad told me Uncle Al had been an anti-aircraft gunner in England during the war. Uncle Al was a roofer when he left for Europe, but when he returned, he couldn't stand on a roof or drive a car. Dad said his jaw was crushed jumping from the anti-aircraft gun to avoid an enemy fighter and his nerves were shot.

~

"Henri, are you ready?" It's Dad coming in the door. "I borrowed John's car and picked up Ruth and Al on the way; are you ready?"

"Yes, we're ready," Mom says as she walks into the kitchen holding me tight.

Dad doesn't look any better than he did earlier and Aunt Ruth has been crying. Uncle Al's the only one who seems okay. Uncle Al says, "Let's go," and starts out the door. As fast as they came in we're out the door and in the car.

Dad asks, "Which hospital?"

"Our … Our Lady," Mom says. Her voice is shaking so much she can barely talk. Uncle Al asks Mom what happened, but she shakes her head. She can't talk.

I wonder what they'll do with me at the hospital. Uncle Al keeps saying I'll be okay. I've never been to a hospital that I can remember. I hope they can fix me.

When we arrive at the hospital, Dad and Uncle Al jump out of the car. Uncle Al opens Mom's door and she starts to get out. She tries to stand, but she's shaking too much.

"I can't get out," Mom says. "My … my legs, I can't."

Uncle Al takes me from Mom and runs toward the hospital. Dad opens the door into the emergency room and Uncle Al puts me on a stretcher. Quickly a nurse starts to push me away. They won't let Dad and Uncle Al follow. They both have tears in their eyes. Uncle Al says, "See you in a little while buddy, be brave." Dad squeezes my hand and smiles through his tears. Our hands pull apart—they're gone.

CHAPTER 2

Several Years Later

⌒

"Come on, Ricky, we're going to be late."

"I'm comin, Ma. Can you tell me more on the bus?"

"Yes, but first we have to get to the bus stop."

It's a cold winter morning and we're late. Mom carries me to save time. We get there just as the bus arrives. Getting on and off the bus is an exercise. Mom says I'm too heavy with my metal leg braces for her to get on the bus while carrying me, so she lifts me while I hold on to my crutches and she puts me down on the first step. Mom steps on the bus and repeats the process until I'm at the top of the steps. I walk down the aisle and find a seat while Mom pays the driver.

"So, Ma, was it a scary day?"

"What day?" Mom's already forgot.

"The day I had polio!"

"Oh, yes, it was very scary for all of us. You were only 20 months old. You were just like your Dad, running every place you went, and suddenly you could only move your arms."

"What happened next, Ma?"

"For you, Ricky, I don't know. The nurse wheeled you away and your Dad and Uncle Al waited to talk with the doctor. When the doctor came out, he said you had polio and you were being transported to the Municipal Hospital. They came back without you and told your Aunt and me what the doctor said. We drove to the Municipal

Hospital and filled out some papers. They said we couldn't see you again until you were released."

"Why did they do that?"

"They said it would best if you didn't see us until you were released."

"Why?"

"Because you can get polio from people who have it; it's contagious. We couldn't be near you, so they said it would be best you didn't see us at all."

"Oh ... what did you do then?"

"We went back out to the car and sat there until it was dark; it was hard to drive away."

"So you didn't see me for a long time?"

"For six weeks. We used to sit outside the hospital every night after your father got home from work and most of the day on weekends. We'd bring dinner or lunch and sometimes both. Aunt Ruth usually came with us. If we had a car rather than the truck and Uncle Al wasn't working, he'd come too. Actually we did get to see you a few times just before you were discharged. You were in an oxygen tent until just before you were released. When you didn't need to be in the oxygen tent, the nurse would take you to the window. You were a long way up, so I don't know if you saw us."

"Did you bring me home when I was done at that hospital?"

"No, they took you to the Weston Hospital for therapy."

"To see Wally?"

"Yes, you've been seeing Wally since the day you left the Municipal Hospital."

Wally's the woman who does my therapy. Mom and I go to see her three mornings a week. She was in the army where she gave wounded soldiers therapy. Wally's a small thin woman like Mom, but she's older. She has light brown hair sprinkled with gray. She always wears a nurse's uniform dress. Wally's a mix of gentle and tough. When she picks me up, she's very gentle, but when we start the exercises, she changes. She never smiles during my exercises and I'm not supposed to complain or refuse. She says it will be long and difficult before we're done, so I may as well get used to it. Mom says I'll be coming here until I'm a teenager. That seems to be forever. Mom says Wally does a great job with me. All I know is it hurts a lot.

"Why didn't I go to the Shriner's Hospital?"

"How do you know about the Shriner's Hospital?"

"I heard Wally talking about it. She said a lot of kids who had polio go there for exercise."

"Yes, that's right. Doctor Derby wanted you to go to the Shriner's Hospital, but your Dad and I wanted you at home. If you went to the Shriner's, you would have gotten your therapy there, but you would also have gone to school and lived there. Doctor Derby said I would have to learn your exercises before you could come home from the Weston. Also, you couldn't hold your head up or sit up when you were released, so Wally wanted to see you every day for a while."

"When could I hold my head up and sit up?"

"You could hold your head up after a couple of weeks, so they let you come home. You sat up on your second birthday, exactly four months after the day you had polio."

"Wow, I didn't know that. When did I get crutches?"

"Not till winter. It took three months for them to make your braces; they always take too long, and then you started learning to walk with crutches."

We get to our stop in the City. Our talking is over; Mom has answered all my questions. We walk to the stop for the city bus. It's so windy. I hate taking the bus in the winter, especially on windy days. Finally, the bus arrives. The doors open and a wave of heat descends on us from the inside of the bus. It feels so good. Mom and I repeat the routine of getting on and as usual the bus is full. I walk to the back of the bus to find a seat.

I'm almost half way through my first year of school. Bob and I couldn't wait to start school. It's not a long walk from home, but it's a lot farther than we've ever been allowed to walk outside the Project before. Now I don't go for therapy three times a week. It's only one time, on Wednesday. It's a small school with only four grades and a lot of the kids in the school come from the Project.

On the first day I saw something I've never seen before. In the back of the classroom there was one boy who was a lot taller than the rest of us. He started to cry the second his mother left. He just kept crying and crying. I've never seen a big boy cry.

"Ma?"

"Yes," Mom answers as she settles in her seat.

"Ma, why did Johnny cry the first day of school?"

"Who?"

"You know, the tall boy."

"Oh yes," Mom remembers, "I guess he was afraid with his mom leaving."

"He's so big, Ma, why would he be afraid?" My voice trails off because I really don't need an answer. What's to be afraid of?

One other thing that's odd in school is the paper. It's brown and there're pieces of wood in the paper. It's hard to write because my pencil gets pushed around by the pieces of wood. I've only seen that paper in school.

We're almost to our stop where it's a long uphill walk to the hospital. Today will be a cold walk with the wind blowing between the buildings and down the street. We arrive at our stop and Mom and I go to the rear steps near our seat; the doors open. This time the wind pushes a wall of cold air into the stairwell of the bus. We descend back into the cold. Mom steps down onto the pavement and turns to lift me to the ground.

Mom's wearing a long coat that's blowing in the wind. The bus driver isn't paying attention as Mom turns to get me. I see Mom reaching for me and suddenly the doors close. The wind has blown Mom's coat between the doors and her coat is trapped. The bus starts to drive away with Mom's coat stuck in the doors! Mom's running beside the bus trying to pull her coat out and stay on her feet. Everyone, especially me, is yelling to the bus driver to stop. It takes him a minute, but he finally stops the bus and opens the doors. I'm shaking so hard. I thought that Mom would fall to the ground and be dragged down the street. I would be alone with a busload of strangers.

When the doors open, I yell, "Are you okay, Ma?"

I can't believe that Mom's still standing; her bag is on the pavement far behind her.

"I'm okay; damn bus driver—he almost killed me."

Mom's never afraid to speak her mind.

Mom's small compared to the other moms. She says she doesn't weigh a hundred pounds. Dad says she's small and shy, but don't cross her. I think the bus driver's lucky we're in a hurry. Mom's most striking feature is her blue eyes. They're all I see when I look at her. Dad says she's very pretty. I don't know; she's my Mom.

Mom has two brothers and five sisters. She says it was hard when she was little. They didn't have much money, but at least my grandparents owned their own home. Before she was even a teenager, Mom and her sisters worked as baby sitters to help support the family. She would often spend the weekend caring for a couple's children while the couple was away. Mom says it was hard to go home and be a child when she had to be an adult on weekends. She says I'll never have to do that.

As we walk away from the bus stop and toward the hill to the Weston, we walk by the diner on the corner. The diner's in the cellar of the office building right by the bus stop. It's just a few steps down into the diner. The windows are at street level and every time we get off the bus, I can smell the muffins and donuts being served inside. I can see the people drinking coffee and eating breakfast. I can see them talking and laughing. They all look so happy. I wish we could stop for a muffin, but Mom always says, "We can't afford that." I know—I've stopped asking.

CHAPTER 3

Parallel Bars

On cold windy days like this, the walk up the street to the hospital seems so steep. I have a hard time walking against the wind. When I lift myself on my crutches and try to swing my legs forward, the wind blows me back. Mom and I are tired by the time we get to the hospital. Walking into the hospital feels so good; it's warm and it smells clean. I feel safe here. I know I'll be sitting down in a little while and Mom gets to have her coffee.

"Hi, Wally."

"Hi, Ricky. Hi, Henri, I've got the coffee ready."

Mom always has a cup of coffee in her hand at home and getting a coffee is the first thing she does when we get to therapy. Wally's waiting for me. I take off my coat and walk into the electric room. There are two hospital beds and two machines in the room. We call it the electric room because the machines have wires that tape to my legs and electricity goes through my muscles. Wally says it stimulates my muscles and nerves, so the exercises work better.

Mom lifts me onto the bed nearest the door, so I can hear her and Wally in the other room while I'm in the electric room. I can read while I'm in here and if the walk is hard like today, I can sleep. The electricity makes my legs tingle, but I've gotten used to it. Wally tapes the wires to me and turns on the machine. To me, it looks like an old machine. It's in a worn, wooden cabinet with white dials and black knobs. If Wally turns the power knob far enough, I can feel the electricity so that it's uncomfortable, but she never turns it up so high that I can't read or fall asleep. There's a newer machine in the room and I've always wondered why I get the old one. There's a girl my age, Becky, who I've seen here a couple of times and she always gets the new machine. I wonder why.

I can hear Mom and Wally talking about the new people in the Project.

"So they wanted to start a petition?" Wally asks.

"Yes, they said they didn't know Ricky had polio before they moved in and they want us to move out."

"What happened?"

"Jean went over and talked to them."

Jean is like Mom; you don't want to tell her no. Jean isn't small like Mom; she's taller and not exactly skinny. I guess the best way to describe her is that she looks like a movie star. When she walks, her long blond hair bounces and she seems to glide rather than walk.

"I couldn't imagine having to leave the Project just after we took Ricky home; that would've been a tough move. We would have had to move back in with Ruth and Al; we can't afford any place else. I can't believe we had to deal with that."

Mom says a few people are afraid that their children will get polio from me, so they want us to leave. She says it's ignorance. They don't understand that I'm not contagious now.

After some time connected to the machine, Wally carries me into the main room and puts me on the low table. The table's the same height as my bed but about twice as big. The pad is covered in vinyl; it's cold on winter days.

I lay down on my back and Wally stands over me. This is the part I hate the most. The first thing Wally does is place one hand on my left knee and place the other hand on top of the hand on my knee. Then she pushes down until the back of my knee touches the pad. Wally talks with Mom all the time about my hamstrings being shortened. She says they need to be stretched every day. I can tell you Mom never forgets. We do this twice every day, even the days we come for therapy. Mom says there's no vacation from my exercises. I know my left leg is slowly getting stronger, very slowly, but the stretching doesn't seem to do anything. The back of my knee never gets any closer to the table.

Mom says my knee never gets any closer because the muscles in the back of my leg are stronger than the ones in the front, so my knee doesn't get straight. Mom says they hope my leg gets straighter as the muscles in the front of my leg get stronger. The stretching hurts a lot. I can feel the pain shoot up the back of my leg. It feels like something, maybe one of those hamstrings, is going to tear outta the back of my leg and shoot across the room.

Wally holds my leg down for a while, then she lets it up. Then she does it again and again and again. I'd like to scream, but it's not allowed. Wally says a tough man doesn't scream or cry and Mom says the men in our family are tough. I know Dad's tough, but I'd like to see them here getting their legs stretched and see if they cry. I guess I'm lucky; I don't have any muscle in my right leg, so Wally doesn't have to stretch it.

After Wally stops the stretching, she exercises the leg. I have to lift my leg up, bend the knee and then straighten the leg. The first time I bend my knee after the stretching, it hurts, but after I bend and straighten it a few times, it starts to feel better. Soon my leg starts to get weak and I can't hold it up or straighten it anymore. Finally, Wally finishes all the exercises with that leg. She does a few exercises with the right leg, but without any muscles we just go through the motions. I know Wally and Mom wish my right leg would start to get some muscle; it's been years, but nothing—not a twitch. Well, except the big toe on my right foot. If I move my big toe on my left foot and I think very hard about moving the big toe on my right foot and you watch my toe very carefully, you can see it twitch just a little bit.

It's cool in the room, but I'm hot. The vinyl on the table is wet with my sweat.

For the last exercises on the table, I lie on my belly with my arms at my side and lift my body up. Then I turn back onto my back and try to do sit ups. I can lift myself up easily when I'm on my belly, but I can't do a sit up. I can get up a little ways, but that's all. Finally, we're done on the table.

Now it's time to walk between the bars. Wally says they're called parallel bars. This is the worst part of my therapy. I put my brace on my right leg and an old shoe on my left foot. Wally says that when my left leg is strong enough I'll have a half brace for a little while and then no brace on my left leg. Someday I'll only have one brace.

I grab my crutches beside me, stand and walk over to the bars. Wally takes my crutches and sits behind me watching. She's watching every step to be sure I'm doing it right. The routine's always the same, walk down between the bars with my right hand on the bar and then walk back with my left hand on the bar."

Walking between the bars hurts as much as stretching my leg. After a few trips up and down between the bars, I'm tired and hurting. I can barely walk two trips between the bars. By the last trip, I can't feel my left leg. It's numb.

"Wally!"

"Yes, Ricky."

"Can we stop now?"

"No," she says in a tone that means *don't ask again*. "Try one more."

When I use my right hand, I take a step forward with my left leg and lift my right leg by pushing down on the bar with my right arm. I pull my right leg forward with my stomach muscles. My leg swings forward. It's hard because my left leg never straightens, so my knee doesn't lock. The muscles in my left knee and butt hurt like a hot poker is being driven into them. Wally says I'm going to have a big butt on the left side because I'm tightening my butt to help the muscles in my left knee keep my leg straight. The thought of a big left butt makes me smile. When I use my left hand, I have to step forward with my left leg then lean forward and slide my left hand along the rail while swinging my right leg forward. Now I'm supposed to put all my weight on my left leg. I can't do it without putting some weight on my left hand. This might hurt more than any exercise. I'm not sure; by this time it's hard to tell.

Finally, Wally says we're done. We have to be done—my left leg is ready to collapse. During the last trip down through the bars, Wally is walking behind me with her hand around my belt; she's ready to catch me if I collapse. I hurt so much. No tears and no complaints, just do it.

I stand at the end of the bars for a moment and walk to the table with my crutches. My left leg is numb and it hurts—if that makes any sense. I can't put any weight on it. Finally, it's time for my snack. I'll rest for a while and then Mom and I will start out to catch the bus home. Mom's anxious to get going. My baby sister Donna is home and Mom always wants to get home to her. As I get my snack, the phone rings and Wally answers it.

"Hello, yes this is Miss Wallington. Yes, Henri's here. Would you like to speak with her? Henri, it's your sister Barbara."

Mom takes the phone with a puzzled look.

"Barbara, what's the matter?" Aunt Barbara's watching Donna.

There's a long pause with Mom listening on the phone. Wally and I wait for her to say something.

"Oh no, I knew this would happen."

"What's wrong?" I ask Mom.

"It's your dad," Mom answers with a pained expression on her face. "His high blood pressure is back."

Mom and Wally look at each other and no one says a word.

CHAPTER 4

A Paper Doll

We rush out of therapy as fast as we left the house this morning. Mom almost forgets her coat.

"Ma, where's Dad?"

"They sent him home from work."

We hurry down the street as fast as my crutches will allow. If Wally saw me walking like I am now, she'd be angry. I don't like to walk this way, but I can't put any weight on my left leg, so I swing both legs forward to take a step, putting my weight on my brace and then swing my crutches forward to take another. Mom's not watching; she's in too much of a hurry. She'd be angry too if she saw.

As we hurry to the bus stop, I don't have much breath left, but I have to ask, "Why is Dad home?"

"Your Dad's headache was so bad, he was sick to his stomach; they want him to see a doctor before he can go back to work."

Dad has had headaches since I can remember. It's always his blood pressure. They discovered he had high blood pressure when he joined the army. He had to lie down for a long time before his blood pressure went down enough for the army to take him. Dad's had a lot of headaches since his new job. He got a job as a machinist at Hamilton where some of my uncles work. Dad said we can afford a lot more now. We have our own car now and we're getting a telephone and maybe even a TV.

19

We're walking by the exhaust fan from the diner near the bus stop. I didn't get to finish my snack and I can smell the hamburgs being cooked in the diner below. I can see the people eating. We'll eat at home.

We arrive home and Dad's lying on the couch. Donna's lying beside Dad sucking her thumb. We always tell her she's going to get buck teeth, but I don't think she knows what buck teeth are. Aunt Barbara's in the kitchen making lunch, grilled cheese sandwiches and applesauce. I listen to Mom and Dad talk while I eat my sandwich and Aunt Barbara picks Donna up to give her a bottle.

"What happened at work today?" Mom asks Dad as she takes off her coat.

"The headache started again and I couldn't stand it anymore, I was sick. I asked the supervisor if I could see the nurse. She took my blood pressure. It was sky high again. She said I needed to go home and call the doctor."

"Did you call?"

"Yes," Dad says quietly.

"What did the doctor say?"

"He wants me to go into the hospital for tests."

Mom gets up and for a moment watches Donna suck on her bottle then goes back to Dad. Dad sits up and Mom sits down. Dad lays back and rests his head on her lap. She strokes his hair.

"Tests? What kind of tests?"

"The doctor wants to check for a brain tumor."

"A brain tumor!" Mom says, her voice rising.

"Yeah."

"When are you going in?" Mom's voice continues to rise.

"Tomorrow morning."

A brain tumor doesn't sound good.

"Barb."

"Yes, Henri."

"Can you take Donna with you when you take Ricky to school?

"Sure."

We finish lunch and bundle up for the walk to school. It's starting to snow outside.

The ground is slippery from the snow. I'm careful not to take too big a step. If I put the crutches and left leg out too far, one of them could slip away from me and if I swing my right leg too far forward, it will slip away. I'm concentrating on walking, but I've got questions.

"Aunt Barb, what's a brain tumor?"

"It's something that grows in a person's brain."

"Is it bad?"

"It can be, but don't worry. Your Dad will be okay."

Aunt Barbara doesn't sound like she believes what she's saying. She looks a lot like Mom. She's younger than Mom, but not by much. I like having her close by. She makes me feel safe; I seem to always know what she's feeling. She can't hide anything from me.

Mom likes to tease Dad that when they got married she had to buy his pants in the boys department and Dad likes to wrestle Mom and kiss her while she laughs and screams, "Put me down!" They play a lot. I don't think there'll be much playing for a while.

Mom and Dad met at a school music festival. She was in her high school senior year; Dad had quit school. With two brothers and three sisters, he needed to work to help support the family. Dad's father, my Pepe, didn't work much, so my Dad had to help.

Mom had a friend who knew Dad and wanted her to meet "this guy." Mom said that when she met Dad she thought he was a jerk. She said he was too full of energy and she was too shy to be near him, but her friend wouldn't give up. Mom's friend made another date for them and this time Mom liked Dad. Mom says the second time it took.

My Dad is special. He's not like other dads; my Dad likes to play with me and Donna. He likes to draw cartoons, especially Donald Duck, and he sings to us all the time. His favorite song is "Paper Doll"; he sings it a lot. It's about a man buying a paper doll that the other fellas can't steal.

Dad knows all the words. He sings to Mom a lot. I like the way she tilts her head and smiles when Dad sings to her.

I know Dad's going to be okay—he always gets better.

CHAPTER 5

Peaches

~

I wish I could stop having that dream. It makes me so sad and lonely every time I dream it. No time to think about it now, Dad's coming home from the hospital today. I can smell the coffee perking downstairs. I can't drink coffee yet. Mom said when I'm a teenager I can start. I wish I was a teenager now; it smells so good. I hope Mom is making oatmeal this morning. It's my favorite, with honey. Aunt Barbara is coming over with Normie and Marty, and Uncle Norm is picking up Dad. Mom says Normie and I can play in the cellar for a little while.

Normie wants to drive the car that Aunt Ruth and Uncle Al got me for Christmas. Well, at least he can if he can reach the pedals. Marty's definitely too small. Mom said Marty's almost in the terrible twos. That must be why he's always bothering Normie and me when we set up the soldiers. Time to get downstairs; I'll put my braces on after breakfast. I'm hungry.

I walk on my knees to the stairs, slide on my butt down the stairs, and walk on my knees to the kitchen. Donna's already in her chair. Mom puts her in the highchair because Donna wanders off if she's not belted in. Mom doesn't want Donna trying to go up the stairs while she's making breakfast.

I can see Mom's making oatmeal. "Good morning, Ma, can I have my oatmeal with honey?"

"Yes, you can."

I climb up in my chair and tickle Donna's feet. She giggles and makes believe she's going to throw her cereal at me. I hope she knows better. If she throws it, her breakfast is over.

"Mom, Dad didn't have a tumor did he?"

"No, he didn't."

"How are they going to make the headaches go away?"

"I don't know yet, Ricky. Your Dad is talking with the doctor this morning before he leaves the hospital. The doctor already told Dad to change his diet. Your father has to have a lot less salt and eat bananas."

"Dad likes salt," I respond. Dad puts salt on his food like its sand on the beach.

Mom says, "Dad's problem is that they used a lot of salt at Dad's house when he was growing up. He likes a lot of salt on his food."

I finish my breakfast and go watch cartoons on TV. Dad bought the TV from the man across the street. He fixes TVs in his store and puts them in the window for sale.

"Ricky."

"Yes, Ma."

"Not too much television. Aunt Barbara will be here with your cousins in a little while and I want you ready.'

"Okay, Ma."

Why can't I stay in my pajamas for a while? Normie doesn't care. So many orders; Dad says it's like being in the army around here. He kids Mom about her being a sergeant.

I climb the stairs to my bedroom and get dressed. I'm brushing my teeth when the doorbell rings. Mom answers the door. It's Aunt Barbara. I can hear Normie ask where I am. Here he comes up the stairs. We'll play up here as long as we can; Marty can't come upstairs. The morning's almost over when I hear the door open. It's Dad and Uncle Norman. Normie and I go downstairs as fast as we can.

"Hi, Dad," I yell as I make my way down the stairs. This time I've got my braces on, so I slide one crutch down the stairs and use the railing and one crutch to lift myself down one step at a time.

Walking on crutches, I can do things a lot of other kids can't. My favorite is to do hand stands on a chair. I put one hand on the seat, the other at the top of the back of the chair and then I lift my body. I can't actually lift my legs in the air. I have to use my left leg to hold my right one from falling forward.

When Normie and I get to the bottom of the stairs, Dad's holding Donna. He picks me up in his other arm and Donna and I hug him at the same time. He smells like the hospital and looks happy and rested. I've been in the hospital so much, I know what it smells like.

"So now you're all better, Dad?"

"Yes I am, Ricky and I'm as hungry as a bear."

Mom's in the kitchen making lunch. Dad puts me and Donna down and walks over to Mom. She's waiting for him. They hug for a long time and Dad kisses Mom.

Aunt Barbara says, "Okay, enough of that."

We kids are having peanut butter and jelly sandwiches and peaches. The adults are having hamburgs. Mom and Dad are standing close together at the stove while Aunt Barbara is making our sandwiches. I hear Mom ask Dad a question.

"What did the doctor say this morning?"

"He wants me to get another job. He doesn't want me to go back to Hamilton. He said it will kill me."

"What are you going to do?"

"I don't know. I heard they're hiring at Builders Supply."

"Doing what?"

"Driving truck."

"That's delivery," Mom says. "It's a lot of heavy lifting!"

"I know, but it pays well; there's a lot of overtime."

Dad puts his arm around Mom and says, "It'll be alright." Mom puts her arms around Dad's neck and holds on tight.

Finally, Normie and I finish our lunch and head downstairs. I love our cellar. The Project is new, so the cellar is clean and bright. It's a little cold in the cellar, but Normie wants to drive the car, so we're going to play down here for a while. The car is made of metal like Dad's, but you pedal it. I can pedal it when I have my braces off, but I can only pedal with one leg. Somebody has to get me started because the pedal won't come back up unless I'm already moving fast. It's easier for me to pedal outside because there's more space to go fast.

Normie tries to pedal, but he can only reach with his toes. I push him around and then we decide to look in the cabinet Dad brought home. It's an old wood cabinet; there might be something fun inside. We find it's empty except for two peanut butter cups. I've never eaten one before. The cups are hard and the peanut butter inside is hard. I find two spoons on the bench and scrape at the peanut butter. Some of it breaks off and I eat it. It doesn't taste bad, but it doesn't taste like I expected it to. I finish mine and see that Normie can't scratch any out of his cup, so I help him. Normie eats just a little. He doesn't like the taste.

I push Normie around for a while and then I start to get a stomach ache. It starts to hurt so much I can't stand up straight and my throat feels like it wants to work in reverse. I walk to the stairs to call Mom—and then it happens. I feel my stomach suck in hard and push everything out. My entire body is shaking so hard I have hold onto the railing or I'll fall. Its peaches—there's peaches on the cellar wall, on the stairs, and all over the floor. Dad hears me and runs down the stairs. He picks me up, runs upstairs and stands me on the floor in the kitchen. He has a towel in his hand and he's catching everything that's coming up. I can't stop it. Dad's holding me tight, so I don't fall back. There's nothing left to come up, but it doesn't stop. Mom's running water in the sink while Dad takes my clothes off. He picks me up and puts me in the sink. Aunt Barbara, Uncle Norm, Normie, and Marty leave quickly for their apartment across the courtyard. Finally, I stop throwing up.

Mom asks, "What happened? Did you feel sick when you went downstairs?"

"No."

Dad goes downstairs to clean up and he comes up with Normie's peanut butter cup.

Dad asks, "Did you eat this?"

"Yes."

Mom asks Dad, "What is it?"

"Ant poison."

Mom looks at Dad and says, "We don't have ant poison. Where …? I thought you said you checked that cabinet!"

Dad just stares at Mom for a minute then says, "I did!"

He didn't—I can tell. I know Mom knows the truth. Dad's tone of voice and the look on his face always give him away. There's a sound of guilt in his voice that he can't hide. I don't know if it's about not checking the cabinet or lying to Mom. Mom can be so tough, especially with Dad. I'm not sure who to feel sorry for.

Mom asks, "Did Normie eat any?"

"He couldn't scratch it out; I did it for him."

Dad starts for the door. "I'll tell Barb and Norm and then we're all going to the hospital."

Normie and I are in the hospital on stretchers, but there's a curtain between us, so I can't see him. They're doing something to Normie that sounds terrible and he's crying, but it sounds strange. It sounds like something's stuck in his throat.

I can't imagine what's happening, so I ask Mom, "What are they doing to Normie?"

"The doctor's pumping his stomach."

"Do they have to pump mine?" I'm panicked.

"No, Ricky, you threw up; Normie didn't."

The relief feels so good. It seems like they're always doing something to me in the hospital. This time I escaped. The doctor tells Mom and Dad that I will have to stay the night in the hospital. That's okay, I like it here most of the time. The only time I don't is at night after visiting time. When Mom and Dad leave, it's lonely. I feel like I do after the dream. The nurse comes in and says they have a bed ready for me. Really a crib, I'm still too small for a bed in the hospital. I don't like the crib. It'll be time for Mom and Dad to leave soon. Mom doesn't seem to be mad anymore.

CHAPTER 6

Cold Feet

Bob and I walk home from school in the snow. This is perfect snow for making snowballs. Bob and I don't have any homework, so we can play for a while before supper.

"Bob, what do you want to do, make a snowman?"

"Let's play house."

"House? No let's make a snowman."

Bob likes to go up to his room where he has a make believe kitchen and make a meal for me and his animals. I think he'll be a cook some-day. Bob has different idears about what's fun. He doesn't like to play war or build snow forts or anything the other boys like to do. I don't mind because I just like being with Bob. We've been friends since I can remember and he knows me better than anyone. My crutch-es don't mean anything to him. I never feel like I'm different when I'm with Bob. If I had a brother, I'd want him to be Bob. Actually, we could be brothers. We both look so much the same. We're both blonds with brown eyes. Bob's just taller. We were both born the same month in the same year.

Today, I think we should make a snowman. Bob agrees. We decide we'll start at the "Big Tree" and push a ball of snow up the hill to the courtyard in front of Bob's. That will make a big bottom for the snow-man. The "Big Tree" is down the hill in the back of the Project. All the boys play down there. The other guys don't like any girls at the

"Big Tree." I wouldn't mind, but I'm not going to tell the other boys except Bob. Bob's like me; he doesn't mind girls being around.

The "Big Tree" starts out as one big trunk and then it splits into three. It's the biggest tree any of us have ever seen. There's so much snow and nobody else is outside; making a snowman will be fun. We've never made a big snowman; we can't wait to start.

I rush into the house. "Ma, Bob and I are going to go down to the "Big Tree" and roll a ball of snow up here to make a snowman."

"Okay, just don't stay out too long. Don't let that leg get too cold."

Mom's always worried about my right leg in the winter. There's no muscle in it, so the blood doesn't flow good. It gets cold easy. Mom says it could get frost bite if I'm not careful. That means they would have to cut off my toes or foot or maybe my whole leg. When I get outside, Bob's waiting. He doesn't look very happy.

"What's the matter, Bob?"

"My mom says we're moving when we get out of school this year."

"Moving? Where are you moving to?"

"To the City. Mom says we're moving closer to where my dad works."

Suddenly it feels much colder and I don't feel like talking or playing, but I don't want to miss this time with Bob. He walks in front of me kicking at the snow. I can't bend my knees with my braces, so Bob's clearing a path. There's still no one else outside now. When we get to the "Big Tree," Bob makes a snowball and starts to roll it toward the hill. I watch because I can't bend my knees, so I can't reach the ball of snow yet.

As Bob's rolling the snowball, it gets bigger and bigger. The ball of snow gets big enough that I can help push. We slip and fall a lot; we're covered with the sticky snow. We look like snowmen! We laugh at each other as we make our way up the hill. I look up at the lights ahead in the courtyard and all I can see is large snowflakes coming down. I can barely see the apartments in all the white. It takes us a long time to get to the courtyard and by the time we get there, it's been dark for what seems like hours. The snowball has become a big ball of snow. It's as high as me. No, maybe higher. I know Mom is going to be mad. I can't feel my right foot, so it's got to be cold. Suddenly I hear Mom's voice in the dark.

"Ricky, where are you?"

"I'm here, Ma. I'm coming."

"See you tomorrow, Bob."

"See you, Rick."

Bob sounds happier. I feel better too, but as I walk toward the steps, I think about Bob not being here. What will it be like without Bob?

When I get in the apartment, Mom helps me with my snowsuit and boots. I know why she's helping. Mom wants to feel that foot.

"Ricky, it's after 5 o'clock. You've been out there for over an hour. Does your foot hurt?"

"No, Ma."

I'm not lying. It doesn't hurt because I can't feel it. That part I'm not going to tell Mom.

"Okay, let's do your bath now to warm that foot."

I knew it. Got to check that foot. Mom can't wait to touch it.

The hot bath is part of my exercises at home. Every night I have to take a hot bath and then we do exercises. It's usually homework, supper when Dad comes home, bath, exercises, story time, and then sleep. Donna and I are in bed by 7:30 every night—even Friday and Saturday night. Mom says we need our sleep. I hate it in the summer when I can hear the other kids outside playing. The sun's still out and Donna and I are in bed. The only good thing is when the moms and dads are sitting outside talking, I get to listen.

We get up to the bedroom and I take my braces off. Mom takes off my right sock. My lower right leg and foot are purple. I'm not surprised. I've seen it purple a lot. The feeling is coming back and it stings a little. Mom doesn't look happy. She touches my foot.

"That foot is as cold as ice. You've got to start coming in when it starts to feel cold."

"I know, Ma."

Mom doesn't seem to be mad at me. I slide off the bed and walk on my knees to the bathroom. The water's still running into the tub. I get up onto the side of the tub and put my left foot in. The water feels good. I lift my right leg up with my hand and slowly put my right foot in the water. It hurts. The water feels like it's on fire. After a few minutes, the sting is bearable and I ease into the water. It feels so good.

Mom comes in, puts the toilet cover down, and sits.

"We made a big bottom for the snowman."

"I know, I saw it," Mom says, "but you stayed out too long."

Mom sounds upset but not at me. I don't know why she gets so upset. My leg and foot are always cold and they get purple a lot. I guess I did stay out too long, but the foot's okay. It's warm and pink now. I have an important question for Mom.

"Ma, why am I so short? Everybody seems bigger than me."

Mom's answer comes without a pause, "God made you small so that it would be easier for you to get around."

That makes sense. I've always known God. I know you can't see him, but I talk to him a lot. Mom says God's everywhere. He can hear you. I'm afraid he can also see me. There's times I wish he couldn't see me. I ask God a lot to make the polio go away. Mom says that's what they call a miracle. I don't know if God has one for me. I'll just keep asking.

I've got another question for Mom, but all I can get out is a whisper. "Ma, do you know Bob's moving away?" I've got my head down; I don't want her to see the tear.

CHAPTER 7

The Nurse

~⁀

"Okay, Ricky, you sleep well and we'll see you tomorrow," Mom says as she and Dad leave. Again I'm in the hospital and with the end of visiting hours the nurses turn a lot of lights off. It's peaceful, but it feels so lonely. You have to experience it to understand. It reminds me of the dream.

This year I've been in the hospital with the measles, mumps, the flu, pneumonia, and a bunch of other things. Mom said I've been home sick or in the hospital more than I've been in school. I've had just about everything a kid can get; next year will be better. Mom says many of the things I had, like the measles, you only get once.

The worst things about being in the hospital are when Mom and Dad leave at night, when I have the dream in the hospital and I wake up even more lonely, when they take me someplace in the hospital and they don't tell me what they're going to do, and when I don't go home when I'm supposed to.

When I had pneumonia, Donna was sick with it too. She came in the hospital a few days after me. Donna went home before me. My fever went away and I was scheduled to go home too, but there was a little boy who's Mom and Dad couldn't visit him. He was crying and I felt bad for him. I know how it feels to be lonely, so I put on my braces and pushed him in a wheelchair. My fever came back.

"Hi, Ricky," Nurse Judy says as she comes up to my bed. They finally decided I can be in a bed.

"Would you like to play in the playroom while I get ready to go home?"

"Okay."

Nurse Judy carries me to the playroom and puts me down on the floor surrounded by toys.

"Just about 10 minutes, Ricky and then it's time to go to sleep."

I play with a truck and soon another nurse I haven't seen before comes to the door and says in a stern, loud voice, "It's time to get to your bed." She walks away before I can say anything.

She's older than Nurse Judy; she seems mad. I put down the truck I was holding and wait for the nurse to come and pick me up.

She comes to the door again and yells at me, "Didn't I tell you to get to your bed?"

As she's saying it she starts toward me. I try to tell her, but she yells, "Get up!"

I try to tell her again, but she bends over, grabs my wrists, and pulls me up to my feet. She lets go and I fall to the floor. Now she's really mad. I'm on my back, and I see that she's so mad her face is as red as a fire truck. She looks like she's going to explode.

She yells, "Why you!"

She's reaching down to grab me again. I'm trying to move away, but I can't move fast enough. Suddenly Nurse Judy comes to the door. She yells, "Mattie, he can't stand; he had polio."

The nurse standing over me suddenly turns white. She looks shocked and without saying a word, she runs out of the room. I feel so bad for her. Nurse Judy comes over and picks me up.

"Are you alright, Ricky?"

"Yes," I reply.

"Is the nurse going to be in trouble?" I ask.

"I'm not happy with her, Ricky. I'll be talking with her about what she did."

"I don't want her to be in trouble," I tell Nurse Judy.

"We'll see, Ricky."

I lay down in bed worrying about the nurse, hoping she won't get in trouble. I promise myself that I won't tell Mom and Dad. The nurse didn't know.

CHAPTER 8

He Always Provides

$\sim$

I'm lying in bed listening to Mom and Dad talk. It's Tuesday night, Mom and I have therapy in the morning, and then right after lunch I'm off to school. Wednesday's are busy; we have to rush from the moment we get up. I get dressed, eat breakfast, run for the bus, take the two buses to therapy, walk up the hill to the hospital, have my therapy, walk back down the street to the bus stop, take two buses home, eat lunch, walk to school for the afternoon part, and finally walk home! I'm tired just thinking about it. Mom says that the tough parts we succeed at prepare us for the challenges ahead. I'm not completely sure I know what she means, but I understand that I have to succeed. Uncle Al likes to say that there's always a way.

"We're going to have to tighten our belt for a while," Dad says to Mom.

"There's not much to tighten. We don't have any more in the bank. We need to get some groceries and I've only got $5.00. How much have you got?" Mom asks.

"Just a couple of dollars; I'll go over to Wieland's tomorrow and pick up what we need."

Wieland's is the little grocery store across the street. There's a garage attached to Wieland's with a gas pump in front. That's where Dad works nights, sometimes pumping gas. There's a little house next to Wieland's where friends of Mom and Dad live. I've never met them, but the girl who lives there goes to my school. She's two years older than me. She's pretty. I'd like to talk to her, but I'm afraid. I love going to Wieland's. The floors are made of wood and they're wavy. It smells like meat in Wieland's, fresh meat.

"Did you see Dick today?" Mom asks Dad.

"Yes, he said he'll know in a couple of weeks."

"They could repossess the car by then," Mom says with her voice raised.

"Did you get a notice?" Dad asks.

"No, not yet, but I expect it any day."

I lay there thinking … what does repossess mean?

"We can't afford to lose the car," Mom says. "You'll never find another job without a car.

"Dick promised something would come up. He gave me my first job; I trust him."

Lose the car? Repossess must mean something about losing the car. I like that car. Dad said it's a great Chevy. It's a lot better than the truck Dad used to bring home. The truck smelled like burned oil. The inside of the Chevy smells good. It smells kind of sweet.

Dad's not been working on Saturday or in the evening. Mom said business has slowed down at Builders Supply, so Dad doesn't get extra time to work. Dad calls it overtime. He says it means more money in his paycheck.

Mom asks Dad, "Would you be delivering parts or working in the machine shop?"

"I don't know; Dick said they're planning on putting a man on the road. They've had to refuse a lot of truck work because they're too busy in the shop to get out. There's a lot of money in doing truck work. Dick said the other guys in the shop aren't interested in working outside in the summer and winter."

"You have to make more money than they pay at Builders Supply," Mom says.

"Dick said it should pay more but not as much as I made at Hamilton."

Mom doesn't say anything for a while. I imagine Dad's holding Mom. He does that when she's sad and she sounds sad. Donna's asleep, but I can't sleep. I want to know more about what's happening.

"We need to pray about this," Mom says.

"About the job and the car," Dad replies.

"Yes, everything," Mom says.

~᛫

I must have fallen back to sleep; it's morning. I hope I didn't miss anything. Dad's on his way to work.

"Hon ..." I hear Mom catch him before he leaves. "Here's $5.00 to get the things we need. Can you bring them home before lunch? We'll need the tomato soup for lunch. I'm also going to make a soup this afternoon with everything we've got left for vegetables and last night's chicken. It'll have to last us the week. When you get paid this Friday, we have to pay the rent. There won't be much left over for food until your next check."

Dad opens the door and says, "I'll need gas too. Yes, I'll be making a delivery not far from here, so I'll stop with the groceries." I hear Dad kiss Mom and the door close. I guess it's time for me to stop making believe I'm sleeping and get breakfast, got to get the bus soon.

~᛫

We're back home from therapy and hurrying across the courtyard. I hope Dad's stayed home long enough for us to see him. Mom's been quiet today. She seems to not be paying a lot of attention to anything, just going through the motions. That's what she says to me when I'm eating and thinking about something else. "Ricky, stop just going through the motions and pay attention to what you're doing." More than once I've spilled something not paying attention. As we approach our apartment, I see Dad's big truck in the parking lot. We walk in the door and Dad's putting Donna in her highchair. It smells like tomato soup in the apartment.

"Oh good, you started the soup," Mom says, kissing Dad as she's taking off her coat. "Did we get anything in the mail today?"

"I've got bad news, Honey," Dad says. "The notice came today from the bank. We've got to the end of the week." Mom just looks at Dad.

"So at the end of the week they come and take the car?" Mom asks.

"I don't know how they do it. I've got to do something before then," Dad says, sounding frustrated.

Now I understand. They're going to take the car. How will Dad get to work? If he gets the job at Auto Gear, he can take the bus because it's close to the place the town bus stops. Dad could ride to work with Mom and me when we go to therapy.

Auto Gear is the place Dad worked when he and Mom got married. Dick was his boss then and now we're waiting to see if Dick has a place for Dad.

"Honey, where's the crackers I asked you to get?" Mom asks.

"That's the other thing," Dad says. "I lost the five dollars. I could only get a few things on the list."

Mom just stares at Dad.

"I'm sorry, Honey; we'll be okay, something will happen."

Mom turns away and takes out the big soup pan and takes vegetables and last night's left over chicken out of the refrigerator. I guess Mom's going to make chicken soup. She's banging things as she works in the kitchen. Mom's mad. Dad has to leave for work, but I see he doesn't want to go. He doesn't like to leave when Mom's mad. Dad finally kisses Mom and starts to walk to the door.

"Goodbye, Son, I'll see you at dinner time. Dad gives Donna a kiss on the top of her head—she's covered in cookie.

"Goodbye, Honey."

"Goodbye." Mom replies. She doesn't look his way. She's not happy. Dad opens the door and leaves.

I can't stand the silence. "Ma, are you making chicken soup?" I know the answer.

"Yes I am; finish your soup. It's time to go to school."

Bob and I are walking home from school, but I'm in no hurry. I know there's going to be a lot of silence around the house for a while.

"Bob, do you hate it when your Mom and Dad are mad at each other?"

"Yes, I go up to my room when that happens; I know I'm next if I'm not careful."

"Me too, I'd like to move to your house tonight until it gets better."

"Why don't you come over to my house when we get home?"

"I'd like to, but I've got to do my homework."

When I walk into the apartment, I can smell chicken. The big pot is on the stove and there's a little bit of steam coming out from under the cover. I sit down at the kitchen table to do my homework while Mom lifts the cover on the pot and stirs the soup. She tastes it and shakes her head. Mom picks up the salt shaker and there's a knock at the door. Mom looks toward the door while she tips the shaker. The top comes off and all the salt falls into the soup. I hear the spoon hit the top of the shaker as she's stirring and Mom hears it too. She looks down and gasps. Then she says to me, "Ricky, get the door." It's Jean.

Mom is spooning soup out of the pot into the sink. Jean asks Mom, "What happened?"

"I tried to add a little salt to the soup and the cover came off." Mom tastes the soup and makes a face. "Ricky is not going to be able to eat this; none of us can eat it. Now what am I going to do?"

Jean puts a book on the table and thanks Mom for letting her borrow it. Mom fakes a smile. Jean says everything will be okay and she quickly leaves.

Mom takes a strainer out of the cabinet puts it in the sink and then she pours the soup into the strainer. She dumps the stuff in the strainer into the pot and goes outside to put it in the garbage. On her way out, Mom says, "Spam tonight." She doesn't sound like she wants to have Spam.

We had Spam last night. I didn't mind. It tastes okay. I can hear Dad's getting ready to go to work. Soon Dad says goodbye, kisses Mom and comes into our room to say goodbye to Donna and me. As usual he runs down the stairs to go to work.

I hear the door open and then Dad yells, "Henri! Henri, come here." Mom runs down the stairs. I have to go. I can't miss whatever is making Dad so excited. I walk on my knees into the kitchen and Dad's bringing food in the door: bread, potatoes, canned vegetables, peanut butter, jelly, and a big container. Mom opens the container and I can smell the soup. It's chicken soup.

Mom asks Dad, "Who left this here?"

"I don't know," he says. "I didn't see anybody."

"Only one person knows I spoiled the soup—Jean. I don't know, should I thank her?"

"No, don't do that," Dad says. "If she wanted you to know she would have just brought it over. Tell her about it and say how wonderful the person is that gave us the food."

Mom says, "I like that."

It was a fun day in school today and I think it was because it's a warmer day, or maybe it's the thought of having chicken soup tonight. Anyhow, it's beginning to feel like spring. We got to go out for recess, which is always a lot more fun than going to the cafeteria and playing on the floor. For me it's a lot more fun to play on the grass. I'm just glad there's no snow or ice. I don't fall much, in fact just once this winter that I can remember, but I'm tired of concentrating on every step. On our way home, Bob and I meet Mom at the mailbox. She's looking at the mail as we walk across the courtyard. Suddenly she stops and stares at one and then she tears it open. She pulls out a piece of paper and says, "Oh my God!" Mom begins to smile like I haven't seen in a long time.

"What is it, Ma?" I'm as excited as she is and I don't even know what it is.

"It's a check, Ricky—a check. It's for a bond I forgot about. It matured. I can't wait to tell your Dad!"

I don't know what a bond is or what matured means, but it has to be good because I know what a check is and it must be ours. I can't wait for Dad to come home.

Mom and I wait for what seems forever for Dad. I can't concentrate on my homework and Donna seems to be getting into everything. Finally, we hear the back door open. It's Dad. Mom walks up to Dad, gives him his welcome home kiss, and gives him the check.

"Where did you get this?" Dad asks. He sounds so surprised.

"In the mail. It's for the government bond we purchased when you were at Hamilton; I forgot all about it. It's not a lot, but we can catch up on our car payments and buy some food."

Dad hugs Mom and swings her around.

Mom says, "We got an answer to our prayers."

CHAPTER 9

A Star

There's a knock at the door; it's Jean. She doesn't wait for an answer. She just opens the door and says, "Rich you've got a phone call; it's Dick at Auto Gear."

From upstairs, Dad yells back, "I'm coming." Barely a foot touches a stair as Dad flies down the stairs and bolts out the door. Mom, Donna, and I are in the kitchen. Mom's making toast for breakfast. I'm excited; I know why Dick is calling.

I have to ask, "Is this about the job?"

Mom says, "I don't know—I hope so."

It was a stupid question, but I can't help myself. Now Mom and I have nothing to do but wait. Anything that seemed important before Jean came in the door is forgotten. Donna is the only one not anxious about what's happening; she's too young to understand. Finally, we hear the screen door open and the door knob turn. It's Dad and he's got a big smile on his face.

Dad walks quickly across the living room floor into the kitchen, puts his arms around Mom's waist, and lifts her up.

"So … did you get the job?" Mom asks, but we already know the answer.

Dad puts Mom down, lifts his arms in the air and yells, "Yes!"

Donna jumps, startled by Dad's yell. She looks like she doesn't know whether to cry or scream. Dad notices and picks Donna up. He starts to dance and sing holding Donna like she's his dance partner.

Mom interrupts the festivities asking, "So what did Dick say?"

"Dick said I will be working on the road. They purchased all the equipment; training starts tomorrow."

"Did Dick mention money?" Mom asks.

"We're going to talk about it tomorrow," Dad says.

Dad sounds happy, but I recognize this line of questioning.

"I wish you asked."

"I did," Dad replied. I could sense his frustration. "He said tomorrow!"

I knew it. Mom can't help herself and I don't know if Dad asked or not. Dad can't seem to remember to get all the information. He gets caught every time. He has that voice and that look again.

"Honey, we'll know tomorrow. Let's be happy."

It's a good argument. I hope it works.

Mom says, "You're right, I'm sorry. Finally, we can maybe catch up."

Whew, Dad escaped this one, but wait, there's more.

"Now don't forget to ask about the insurance and …"

Dad interrupts Mom, "Things are going to be okay. Now—how about that toast?"

After breakfast I learn more good news. Saturday Uncle Al, Dad and I are going to the VFW in Westside to collect for the March of Dimes. I love going to collect. Dad says we do real good because Uncle Al is a wounded veteran and the men there can't say no to me. I like going because I love the smell in the VFW and the clubs where we go to collect. Dad says it's the smell of stale beer. I can smell it on my clothes after we leave. I'm also looking forward to Saturday night because I get to stay over at Aunt Ruth and Uncle Al's apartment when we collect. Uncle Al usually has to go to work and I like watching television with Aunt Ruth and keeping her company.

It's so peaceful in their apartment at night. They live on the fourth floor in the City and I can see the cars on the main street out the window from my bed. I can also see the neon lights from the liquor store at the end of the street. Uncle Al and I go there to buy his beer.

Sometimes we go shopping for groceries, or he will buy me a shirt or a pair of pants. Last time we went out Uncle Al bought me a rabbit and a cage. I was going to take the rabbit home and he was going to be my pet, but Mom made Uncle Al take the rabbit back. She said we had no place to keep him. Mom did let me keep the parakeet we got instead; we call him Ricky Boy. As usual, Uncle Al winks at me and says, "There's always a way."

Uncle Al is like no one else in the family. I know he's not a lot older than my Dad, but he seems older. Maybe the war made him older. Uncle Al always wears a dress shirt and pants. Even if we're on vacation together, Uncle Al is wearing his best. He's darker than the rest of us even though he's French like my Dad's family. He has black hair and his skin looks like he has a constant tan. Uncle Al must have short arms because he's the only man I know who wears elastic bands around his upper arms to hold his sleeves up. There's something else about him, he's the most gentle man I know. My Dad's gentle, but Uncle Al is even more gentle. I like being with him.

It's very late and I'm in bed looking outside. It looks so lonely on the main street at night. I see people walking alone headed for the liquor store, and I see cars drive by that I imagine people are driving alone. I never liked the feeling of loneliness, but I'm getting used to it. It's only when I have the dream that I feel a loneliness I can't get used to. It consumes me; I feel it in every part of my body and mind. All I see in the dream is what looks like the front of a building. I don't know if the building exists; maybe it does or maybe only in my mind. And, why such a powerful, consuming feeling of loneliness? It doesn't help that Uncle Al works nights. When I'm here, I lay awake waiting for him to come home.

Consume or to be consumed—we learned the word in school recently. Mrs. Clark said it's a good word to know because it's one of those words that no other word will do. Mrs. Clark says we consume food, meaning we eat it, and if we have an emotion like happiness or fear and we say we're consumed by it. That means it affects us completely. I guess I can use it with being lonely.

Monday Marty's going into the hospital to have his tonsils out. Mom says your tonsils are in your throat. They get infected and the doctor has to cut them out. The good thing is that you can eat a lot of ice cream after until your throat doesn't hurt. I wouldn't want anybody cutting something outta my throat no matter how much ice cream I got to eat. Uncle Al finally comes home from work. I fall asleep and have no dreams.

Today is Monday. All of us guys finished our homework and headed down to the "Big Tree" and played war for the rest of day. There's a new boy, Jerry, whose family moved into the apartment next to us. He always plays too rough. I think he's what you'd call a bully. Except for Bob, Jerry scares the other kids because he's bigger. Bob never seems to be afraid of anything. It isn't that he's the biggest or toughest, he just doesn't seem to be afraid—even when he knows he's going to get spanked. I wish I could be like Bob. I'm not afraid of Jerry either, but I don't like the idear of getting hurt.

Jerry says he's going to pick the teams, but it's not his turn. He says to all of us, "I pick or else."

"Or else what?" I ask Jerry.

"Or else I'm going to beat up everybody here."

He says it like he's going to enjoy beating us all up. I've had enough. It's not fun playing since Jerry moved in. Then Jerry pushes Bob. Without even a thought, I jump at Jerry and put my arms around him. He's bigger than me, but I caught him off guard, so he stumbles to the ground. I'm stronger than all the boys. I'm smaller, but walking on crutches makes me stronger. I guess that's a good thing.

Dad gets me in headlocks when I wrestle with him; I've had enough of them to know how to do it and I get Jerry in one. It wasn't hard. I've never wrestled with Jerry, but I can feel that I'm stronger. He keeps trying to pull his head out, but I've got him good. He can't get his head out without losing his ears. During the depression when Mom was a little girl, Mom's dad, my Papa, was a wrestler. Papa has what Mom calls cauliflower ears from all the headlocks he got. Papa wrestled traveling wrestlers who came into towns to challenge the locals. The wrestlers got paid and the men who stayed in the rink long enough got money. Mom said Papa was tough and he stayed in long enough many times.

I'm ready to give Jerry cauliflower ears. "Okay, Jerry, are you going to give up?"

"Yes, let me go!"

I let him go and he runs away.

A few minutes later I hear Mom calling. I hope I'm not in trouble. "I've got to go guys. I'll see you later."

When I get home, I see Mom looks like she's been crying. "What's the matter, Ma?"

"I'll tell you later, Ricky. Dad's coming home; we're going to Nana and Papa's."

Mom goes upstairs and brings down bags with clothes in them.

"Ma, where are we going?"

"You're staying at Pepe's tonight and Donna's staying at Aunt Ruth's.

"Why?" I ask.

"We'll talk about it later when your Dad gets home."

Now I'm worried. It must be bad if Mom's been crying and she won't tell me why. Finally, Dad comes in the door. Mom and I are sitting on the couch and Donna's playing on the floor. Dad kisses Mom and sits on the floor at Mom's feet and looks at me.

"Son, something bad happened today."

I look at Mom and see her jaw is shaking; she's trying not to cry.

My stomach starts to hurt—what does this mean to Donna and me? I'm afraid that something terrible is going to happen to our family. I don't know why, but I feel like we're never going to be together again. Every time I get scared about something that upsets Mom and Dad, I think I'm going to have to go away.

Dad continues, "Marty died today at the hospital."

Died! Marty? What did he do? He wasn't old or real sick. I've been sicker than him.

"What happened, Dad?" I've got to know.

"They couldn't stop the bleeding during his operation. He died."

"So he won't come home?"

"No, Ricky, he won't," Mom says. "He's with God."

We're all at Nana and Papa's; all my aunts and uncles from Mom's side and most of my cousins are here. Aunt Barbara's in the kitchen crying. Mom, my other aunts, and Nana are with her. Dad, Uncle Norm, Papa, and my other uncles are outside on the porch. They're talking quietly, so I can't hear them. Donna and I and our cousins are packed in the living room with instructions to sit quietly, not to talk. Fred and I and our cousin Howie get up from the floor and walk to the window. Not exactly what we're supposed to be doing but there's really no room to sit. Our moms said that when a child dies a new star is born.

It's dark now and the three of us look out the window up at the stars. We don't talk; we know what we're looking for. I've never noticed there were so many stars. I look at Howie and he seems to have as many freckles as stars in the sky. The good part about being here tonight is being with all my cousins, especially Fred. I always feel better when I'm with Fred.

Well, it's not just Fred. Little Leota and I share something special too. We both had polio. She got it a week after me. You'd never know she had it because all of her muscles work. The only thing she can't do is run. She tries, but she trips over her own feet. She can walk fast, but she can't run. We have always been very close. I sometimes feel sad for her because she often acts like she's broken. It's as if she feels she's different because she had polio. I don't know how she could feel that way because to look at her you'd never know it. She's the most beautiful girl I know. She looks like a model. I know it sounds weird but we asked our Moms if cousins could get married and they said no, it's against the law. It doesn't matter, we'll always be close. I look back at her and see she's playing with Donna. Donna's too young to understand.

Dad comes in the house and goes into the kitchen. I hear him say, "It's time to get the kids to Dad's and Ruth's."

We're in the car and Mom and Dad aren't saying anything.

I ask Mom, "Where's Normie?"

"Normie's with a babysitter." I can't imagine losing Donna.

We're at Pepe's now and Dad stops the car. I'm still looking up at the stars.

"Will we ever see Marty again?"

"Someday," Mom answers, "when we go to heaven."

I dream about the building again. I wake up and look out the window at the stars. I feel so alone. I wonder if Marty's lonely, if he's consumed.

CHAPTER 10

A Phone

It's finally summer and we've been out of school for over a month. Today was a boring, rainy day. It's evening now and as it's the summer, it's still light out and Donna and I are in bed. There're only two bedrooms, so I have to share a room with Donna. Donna always falls asleep and I lay here daydreaming. Mom says I spend too much time daydreaming. Sending me to bed when it's light out doesn't help. Tonight no one's outside for me to listen to, so I've got a lot of time to daydream. I've been thinking about Marty. He never did anything wrong, so it doesn't make sense. Mom says a lot of things don't make sense to us, but they do to God. She said God wanted Marty to be with him; it was part of God's plan. I wish I knew His plan. I wonder if polio was part of God's plan.

Bob moved away last week. He said he'd have his own bedroom in their new house. Some of the other boys who lived in Bob's building, Brian and Ronnie, moved away too. There aren't many boys my age here anymore. Mom said this could be our last year in the Project. Yesterday I played with some of the other boys. I never played with them much before, but they're the only ones my age. Jerry was in trouble as usual, so he had to stay in the house. Ever since Jerry and I had the fight, we've been friends. Not nearly as close as Bob and me but friends. It might be because there's so few of us left.

Something bad happened here yesterday that I'm not sure I understand. There was a bird nest in a bush near the building across the courtyard. There were baby birds in the nest and two boys I barely know, they're older, were looking at the baby birds. I went over to see what the boys were looking at. One of the boys knocked the nest to the ground and they beat the baby birds with sticks. The boys got real excited and ran around the courtyard. Finally, the boys got tired and started to sit down in the grass, but one of the boys saw a baby carriage outside an apartment two doors from mine.

I heard one of the boys say, "Let's go see if there's a baby in there." They went over and I had to see. There was a baby sleeping in the carriage. The boys started yelling and the baby started to cry. I couldn't believe it. Why were they doing it? I suddenly realized that I had this odd feeling of power over this little baby. For some reason, I liked the feeling but at the same time it scared me. Suddenly, a woman who I never saw before came out and asked what we were doing. The other boys ran. I couldn't run fast enough to get away. I just stood there.

"What are you doing to my baby?" I couldn't talk. She ran down the steps of the apartment and picked up the baby and yelled in my face, "What were you doing to my baby?"

Mom looked out the door and asked what happened. I told the woman and Mom that the boys woke the baby and the baby cried. Mom said it was time for me to come in. I don't understand the feeling I had. I can still feel it when I think about it. It's got to be wrong. I've got to get to sleep; tomorrow morning we're getting a phone. I asked Mom if I could call Bob when we get the phone. She said maybe. I've got to go to sleep.

It's morning and the phone man's finally here. He's a nice man. I watched him use a screw driver to attach a little box to the molding near the floor at the bottom of the stairs that go to the bedrooms. He attached the wires from the phone to the box then went down into the cellar to do some more work. He's back and picked up the phone. He said it works. The man held the phone to my ear; it makes a burr sound. He gave Mom a big book and told her it had names and phone numbers.

"It has a great cast but not much of a story," he said.

Mom laughed. I didn't hear him say anything funny. Mom thought it was funny. Well he's finally picking up his tools and leaving. Wow, we have our own phone!

"Ma, can I call Bob?"

"No, we're going to have lunch now."

I can smell the grilled cheese sandwiches cooking and I'm hungry, but I'm disappointed. I can't wait to call. We finally finish eating and I ask if I can call now.

Donna and I have to take a nap every afternoon after lunch and I'm afraid Mom's going to say no not till after my nap, but she says, "Okay, but first you have to look up his number in the book the man gave us."

It's a blue book with a picture of the City on the cover. The book is floppy and heavy. It's hard to hold, so I lay it on the floor near the couch and start looking.

Nothing in the book makes sense, so I ask Mom, "Can you help me find his number?"

Mom sits on the couch and looks down at the book. "First you have to find Bob's last name. I look through the book until I find his last name and Mom says, "Now you find Bob's dad's first name next to his last name. His name is Hubert."

I didn't know that. We always called him Hub. I find Hubert and there's Bob's new address. They must know everything at the phone company. Next to Bob's address is a bunch of numbers. Mom tells me to write them on a pad she hands me and we go over to the phone. I think the phone's in a funny place on a little table at the end of the stairs. If you want to sit down when you're on the phone, I guess you'll have to sit on the stairs.

Mom says, "Now put your finger in the hole for the first number and turn the dial clockwise until you can't go any further and take your finger out. When the dial turns back, dial the next number until you've dialed all the numbers. You'll hear a ringing and, if anyone is home, they'll pick up the phone and say hello. You answer back hello, say who you are, and ask for Bob."

It's not easy to dial the phone. This is my first time dialing. I don't know what I'm more excited about, using the phone or calling Bob. I finish dialing and the phone's ringing. Now I'm so excited I'm shaking.

The phone stops ringing and I hear Jean say, "Hello."

I can't believe it. I hear her voice on the phone. "Hi, Jean, this is Ricky; is Bob there?"

She says, "Ricky is this really you—so you got a phone?"

"Yes, is Bob there?"

"Yes he is, Ricky; I'll get him for you."

I can't believe it. It's been weeks since I talked to Bob.

"Hi, Rick." It's Bob.

"Hi, Bob!" I almost yell into the phone.

We talk for a while about the new kids he met, especially Elaine and Wendy. Bob said Elaine has asthma. I know what asthma is because Mom told me about it. She told me she had it until she was 14. Elaine can't run or play hard because her asthma's real bad.

"Bob, where do you go to school?" I ask.

"I go to Saint Mary's."

"Saint Mary's? That sounds like a church. You go to school at church?"

"Kind of," Bob said. "It's a parochial school at the church. We have nuns for teachers"

Bob told me about nuns before. They're the only people he's very careful around. He said that at church if he ran he could get a whack. They weren't afraid to hit him right in front of his mom. I decided I was happy I didn't go to school with Bob.

We finally run out of things to talk about. I say goodbye and Mom asks to talk to Jean. When Mom hangs up the phone, she says I can go and visit Bob in two weeks. I'm too excited to sleep, but Mom says it's nap time. More rest. I think rest time is for Mom. I wonder if God has a last name. Can't look Him up in the phone book without it.

The summer's almost over and it's been slow, not much to do. I can't wait to go back to school and for Cub Scouts to start. The woman across the courtyard, Bessie, is our den mother. Bessie's children are all grown up and her husband died, so she lives alone. She's older than Mom; Bessie's like a grandmother to us. I know she looks forward to us coming over to her apartment to make crafts.

Bessie played a trick on me at the 4th of July parade. Our pack got to walk in the parade and I couldn't wait to march in my uniform. When we got to the place where the parade would start, Bessie had a wagon with the name of our pack, written on cardboard, attached to the side of the wagon. Bessie said I was going to get the chance to hold onto the signs during the march to make sure they didn't fall off. She wasn't fooling me; I knew what she was doing. She didn't think I could march all the way to the end, so she was trying to make it easy for me. I was going to say no, I would walk, but I didn't want to hurt Bessie's feelings. She was trying to be nice.

The summer wasn't much fun because the other guys have bikes and no one goes down to the "Big Tree" anymore. When we were little, we all had tricycles. Dad nailed some of my old shoes to the pedals so I could keep my feet on the pedals. I could only pedal with my left leg but once I got started, I could keep up. We couldn't go far anyways. If I tipped the bike over, I didn't fall off. I was attached to the bike. I would just push myself and the bike back up. Then the other guys started riding two wheel bikes and I was getting too big for my left leg to move me. My leg just isn't getting strong enough. I wouldn't be able to keep up with the guys on the two wheel bikes anyways. At least we don't use bikes at Cub Scouts.

At lunch today, Mom said she and Dad have a surprise for me and Donna, but we have to wait until Dad comes home. I can't wait. The day seems so long, but finally the door opens and it's Dad. I love it when he gets home. I love the smell of his uniform. He smells like Auto Gear. It's kind of a sweet oil smell. The smell makes me feel good; it makes me feel safe.

Dad crouches down and hugs me and Donna and then we both yell, "What's the surprise?"

Dad looks up at Mom, smiles and says, "We're all going with Uncle Al and Aunt Ruth to see Roy Rogers and Dale Evans this weekend at the coliseum. Uncle Al bought tickets for all of us."

Donna and I are so excited. Donna's jumping around screaming. I can't wait—I have to know.

"What day, Dad?"

"Saturday, Saturday afternoon," Dad says.

Today's Tuesday; tomorrow I go for therapy and then Mom and I have to see Dr. Derby. Just two days after that is all that's between me and seeing Roy Rogers. Dad works Saturday morning. He says after work he's going to pick up Uncle Al and Aunt Ruth; we'll have lunch and then go to the coliseum—wow!

CHAPTER 11
Life's Heroes

~⌒~

Therapy is over. I'm tired and I hurt, but the graham crackers and milk I'm going to get in a minute and the thought of seeing Roy Rogers make up for it

"Well, Ricky, would you like a surprise?" says Wally as she gives me my crackers and milk.

"Yes," I respond. A big smile comes across her face

"What's the surprise?"

Wally says with as much excitement as I feel, "Ricky, you're doing so good walking between the bars and up the stairs that today you're going to be fitted for a half brace on your left leg. You know what that means don't you?"

"I do, I do!" I almost scream out. "I can bend my left knee all the time."

"That's right," she says.

I know exactly what that means. Up to now, when I walked up stairs I had to put both crutches on one side and use the railing to lift myself up high enough to get my feet up to the next step. Going down I reverse that. Now I'll be able to bend my left knee and put my left foot up one step then use my crutches and left leg to get up another step. It isn't a lot easier than lifting myself with just my arms, but it's safer. It's not easy balancing myself when I'm lifting both of my feet at the same time. Now maybe I can walk up to Aunt Ruth and Uncle Al's apartment on the fourth floor without any help.

For months now I haven't been going into the electric room. Wally said I didn't need to anymore. Now I exercise the entire time I'm here. It's hard, but I know I'm getting stronger. Today I'm shaking as I eat my crackers and milk. I'm so hungry I could eat the whole box of crackers. Wally sees me shaking and gives me another cracker. It's going to be a little while before I'll be ready to go. I really want to go because the sooner we get to Dr. Derby's the sooner the day ends and we're that much closer to seeing Roy Rogers.

Finally, I've stopped shaking and we're leaving. I wish Mom could learn to drive. Many years ago, when Mom was a girl, she hit her mouth on the dashboard in Papa's car when another car hit them. Mom's teeth got bad so they took them out and Mom got false teeth. I think that's what made her afraid to drive. I remember Dad getting her to try once on a road with no cars. Mom drove a little ways, but a dog ran in front of the car and Mom stopped quickly. Donna and I slid off the seat onto the floor and Mom said, "I'm never trying that again."

The walk down the hill to Dr. Derby's seems to take forever. It's twice as far as the bus stop and the hill is much steeper. I wonder if it will be easier when I only have one long brace. I can't wait to see. Finally, we walk into the little lobby of the building where Dr. Derby's office is. The walls of the lobby are made of shiny stone that's white and gray. The ceiling is made of brown metal tiles. The elevator is real old with a door and a gate. Behind the elevator is a room where they make my braces. I guess Mom and I will go in there today. Mom pushes the button for the elevator and there's the loud sound of the elevator when it starts to move. The wait seems so long. Finally the elevator arrives; the door opens and Mom opens the gate. We step on and the process is reversed.

Dr. Derby is on the second floor. The elevator slowly rises from the lobby to the second floor. There's a small opening in the side of the elevator where I can see a brick wall slowly passing by, brick by brick. We finally make it to the second floor. Mom and I walk into the Doctor's waiting room. It's a small room, longer than our living room but about as wide. At the far end of the room on the wall to the right is a desk in the corner, and the woman who works for Dr. Derby, Martha, is sitting at the desk. On the same wall but on this end of the room is the door to the room where Mom and I see Dr. Derby, the examination room. Around the room are fancy, uncomfortable, wood chairs to sit on.

The room is only lit by the small lamp on Martha's desk and two tall lamps between the chairs. Mom says hi to Martha and sits on a chair next to one of the lamps. There's no window in the room. The wallpaper and pictures in the room look very old. The pictures are small and they're not really pictures. They're drawings of old doctors, at least I think they're doctors, in black suits, high hats and long beards. I sit next to Mom and smile at Martha. She smiles back. She always says hi to me.

Mom and I have been coming here for six years and I've never heard Martha say more than 10 words while we were waiting. Most of the time Mom and I have to wait to see the doctor for over an hour. Sitting here is very difficult. It feels like it's evening in the room and it's so quiet that I don't like to even talk to Mom. We whisper when we talk. At least I get to read.

Finally, Martha tells us the doctor's waiting. We enter the examination room. This room is the same size as the waiting room, but it has two windows so it's very bright. There's a high table made of dark wood and dark brown leather in the center with a step stool that I sometimes use to get on the table. The leather is always cold on the table. There're several chairs and cabinets in the room and more doctor pictures on the walls. These walls are painted light blue. It's definitely a brighter room than the waiting room.

Dr. Derby walks in and says hi. He's got my big folder and a pen in one hand. He shakes Mom's hand and sits down in front of me. Dr. Derby is a very tall man, but as Mom says, as skinny as a rail. He's much older than Mom, in fact, he reminds me of President Lincoln.

He has thinning, grey hair and an aging face, but he walks like a young man. Dr. Derby has giant hands, which when he lifts me, seem to wrap around my entire body. He smiles often, but it doesn't seem to be because he's happy, it's to be friendly.

"Well, Ricky, how's school?" Dr. Derby asks.

"Fine."

"How are your grades?"

I know what he's asking. This part I hate. I know I can't hide anything from the doctor; Mom's sitting right there. "Not too good," I answer.

Mom says, "Mostly C's."

Dr. Derby gives me that look again. I'm not very proud of myself. He doesn't say much; I wish I could just once say my marks are good.

Dr. Derby looks at Mom and says, "He's missed a lot of school. They should probably keep him back in the next year or two."

Mom nods her head, yes. I know what they're talking about, but I'm not going to say a word. Mom has told me more than once that I only speak when spoken to and Dr. Derby isn't asking my opinion. I wish I could tell him how hard it is to always be playing catch up.

"Henri, have you noticed whether Ricky's right foot is slightly smaller than his left."

"Yes," Mom says.

Doctor Derby continues: "This is going to become more pronounced over the years. The reduced circulation in his legs will cause both of his legs to be shorter and both of his feet smaller than they would have been if he didn't have polio, but the diminished growth will be most pronounced in his right leg and foot. It's time to have his feet checked to see if he needs two different size shoes. Here's the name of a local shoe store that I trust. They'll sell you two pairs for a reduced rate. You'll only pay one-half for the second pair. Ah yes, one more thing. When you leave here I want you to go right downstairs and get fitted for the half brace for the left leg and a new brace for the right leg with a knee lock. Ricky, you're getting too tall not to be able to bend your knees when you sit."

I can't believe it—new shoes and two new braces and I'll be able to bend both knees when I sit—wow!

Dr. Derby lifts me out of my chair and sits me down on the cold, leather. I can feel the cold through my pants. I take my pants and braces off and lay down, now I'm very cold. The doctor examines my legs and does some of the exercises I do with Wally including those for my stomach and back. Never during this time does he smile. Finally, he sits me up and I get dressed. While I'm dressing Dr. Derby sits and writes notes.

When he finishes with his notes, he turns to Mom and says, "It's slow going, but Ricky's getting stronger in that left leg and yes, it's time for a new pair of shoes." Dr. Derby stands, lifts me off the table, and sets me on the floor. We're headed downstairs for my brace fitting.

The fitting is done and we're leaving the building. Mom says we're going to go see Dad at work. I'm hungry again. I ate a peanut butter and jelly sandwich during the fitting, but walking by the restaurant on the way to Dad's work makes me hungry. I can smell hamburgs. It seems like that's all I can smell here in the City. Well except for the exhaust from the buses. Mom never has to eat; all she needs is coffee. It's getting late, so Mom says we can go home with Dad. I can't wait to get to Auto Gear. Mom can't wait either; John always gets Mom a coffee when we arrive. Finally, we arrive and there's Dad and John standing by the big door that leads into the shop. John smiles a big smile and says hi.

"So how you doing, Ricky?" John says as he lifts me up with his big hands.

I love to see John. We have something in common. John says neither of us can hide in a crowd. John has dark skin and I have crutches. There're a few other people in the City with dark skin like John but not many. I'm the only person I see with crutches. I like being the only one, but I don't like it when strangers try to help me. They get so excited and noisy about it.

"Oh, let me get that door for you."

"Oh, let me carry that for you."

They say it so loud and everybody looks. I'm small, but I can do it myself.

John's the biggest man I know. He looks like he could pick all of us up at the same time. Dad and John have been friends ever since Dad started to work at Auto Gear. Dad said John taught him everything he knows. John never treats me like I have a problem. People talk to me like I'm sick or I don't understand. Not John, he's like my friends and family. They don't treat me different.

Mom tells Dad what Dr. Derby said and that they will have to buy two pairs of shoes for me from now on. She also says they'll only be able to afford to buy me the two pairs. So I can only have one pair of shoes.

Dad says, "What's he going to play in?"

"He'll have to be careful," Mom says.

I don't care; I just can't wait to get new shoes.

Dad says, "Thank God the March of Dimes pays for the braces."

John takes me over to the bench to see an automobile cylinder head he's working on. It's as big as me and made of metal. John picks it up, carries it over to the cleaning tank and asks me, "Well, Ricky, would you like to clean the head?" John and Dad laugh. I hope that means I don't have to clean it. I can't get up that high.

The day has finally arrived and we're on our way into the coliseum to see Roy Rogers. The coliseum is a big building made of wood that looks very old. I know it's old because Papa used to wrestle here when Mom was a little girl. Inside you can walk all the way around the building and there're no corners. It's like going around in a round tunnel. The outside wall has all the doors coming in and the inside wall has places where they sell food. We walk around until we get to where our seats are. Uncle Al's carrying me. We walk into the area they call the arena.

The stairs leading to the seats are made of wood; they're worn from all the people walking on them. The seats are made of wood too. There's a wood fence all the way around the arena with wide gates on either end where you can get into the arena. We get to our seats and sit down. There're so many people here.

Uncle Al gets us all sodas and then music starts playing and a man is talking on the speakers. I hear him say, "Let's all stand to welcome Roy Rogers." Uncle Al picks me up and starts to go down the stairs. The man is still talking, "King of the Cowboys."

"Where are we going, Uncle Al?" I ask.

"You'll see," he says.

I'm trying to see Roy, but it's hard. There's so much excitement; everyone is trying to see him and Dale. When we get to the bottom of the stairs, I can see him. I can't believe it; Roy Rogers right there in our arena. He's slowly riding to the center of the arena waving his cowboy hat in the air. Dale Evens is following right behind him. I start to wave as Uncle Al turns and walks to the gate on the other end of the arena from where Roy came in. There's a guard there. Uncle Al tells the guard something and shows him a paper. I can't hear him with the music and noise of the crowd. The guard looks at the paper, nods his head yes, and opens the gate. Uncle Al and I walk right into the arena and Uncle Al walks toward Roy Rogers and Trigger. He walks right up to Roy Rogers and Trigger and tells Roy my name.

Roy Rogers puts his hand out and says, "Howdy partner."

I shake his hand—I can't believe it! I don't see or hear anything else in the coliseum; just Roy Rogers and Trigger. How did Uncle Al do this? I'll never forget this day!

CHAPTER 12

Blueberry Hill

Bob's standing at the curb as we drive up. Mom, Dad, and I get out of the car. I get my suitcase and we walk toward Bob's house. Finally, I'm visiting Bob at his house. Bob lives in a big house, unlike the apartments in the Project. There're a lot of kids running around and one skinny girl with a whole lot of freckles and red hair sitting on the steps.

"Hi, Rick," Bob says.

We walk toward the girl and Bob says, "This is Elaine."

Elaine says hi, gets up from the steps, and walks over to us.

"You're Bob's friend, Rick," she says.

It isn't a question, it's a statement. How'd she know? She must have heard Bob say hi to me.

"Yes," I respond, which seems a little silly since she didn't ask me a question.

I've never seen anyone with as many freckles or with red hair. I can't help staring at her. She looks like she could burst into flames at any minute. Bob takes my suitcase from me, tells Elaine we'll see her in a little while, and we go into the house.

Bob lives on the second floor and Elaine lives on the first. They have a big kitchen and dining room, a living room, a bedroom each for Bob and his little brother Stevie, a big bedroom for Jean and Hub, and a front and back porch. Bob's bedroom is so big he has a double bed like Mom and Dad. Bob puts my suitcase on his bed and we go back outside. Stevie hasn't left us alone since I got here and as usual he's coming outside with us. He can be a pain.

When we were still in the Project a bunch of us were playing cowboys and Indians and Stevie hit me on the forehead with the butt of his plastic gun. I started to bleed like someone turned on a faucet. The blood ran down my face and onto my clothes. In minutes my shirt was covered with blood. Mom and Dad ran out of the apartment, picked me up, and we all piled in the car and headed for the hospital. The last sound I heard was Jean spanking Stevie and him screaming. Now if we could just find a way to get him in trouble today. Bob decides he's had enough.

"Mom, Stevie's bothering us."

Jean comes quickly and drags Stevie, kicking and screaming, into the house.

Elaine is still on the porch and asks if we want to play Chutes and Ladders.

Bob says, "Okay."

Elaine seems so delicate, she would break if you bumped her. Bob told me that sometimes Elaine has a hard time breathing and she has to take medicine. Sometimes she has to go to the hospital. Sitting on the porch playing, I can't help listening to Elaine, listening for her to have trouble breathing. It makes me nervous. I think she has a harder time than me. I can't imagine not being able to breathe. Bob says Wendy's not home this weekend; I'll see her next time. Bob says she's a lot of fun, a little wild. I'd like to see that.

We spend the day playing with Elaine and finally Jean calls us for dinner. Mom and Dad have left and after dinner Bob and I sit on the front porch talking. It's long past my bedtime at home. Bob and I talk about everything and when we go to bed, we continue talking. I miss having Bob nearby. Talking on the phone's not the same. After talking for hours, we finally fall asleep, but soon I wake up with that feeling of loneliness. I dreamt about the building—I don't know where I am! For a minute, I think I'm lost someplace; my heart's pounding hard enough for me to hear and feel in my ears. Then I hear Bob breathe and remember where I am. Everything's okay—I fall back to sleep.

~

It's taken forever to get them, but we're here and I've got the new braces on. We bought my new shoes months ago and I'm finally getting to wear them. Every two weeks Mom and I came here for a fitting and every time it seemed like they hadn't done anything since the last time. Mom told the man I would outgrow the braces before I got them. He didn't say much and he's not saying much now either; he never does. He always chews on a toothpick. He probably doesn't talk because he's afraid he'll drop or swallow the toothpick. I like the smell here; the smell of oil and leather. It's kind of a messy place. Every time we come the man has to clear papers and magazines off the table where I sit for the fitting. The paper is from a big roll. He uses the paper to trace my legs. There're papers with tracing all over the room.

The man clears the table, so I can sit and put the new braces on. A half brace on the left leg and a full brace on the right that I can unlock and bend. This feels so strange. My knees are bent and I've got my braces on. The man shows Mom something else new. My other braces were attached to the heels of my shoes so we couldn't easily change my shoes. Now we can. There's a metal tube that goes through each of the heels and at the end of the braces the ends bend in and stick into the tubes. It's great, but I doubt we'll ever get to use them. My shoes are expensive. I lock the knee on my right brace, put my crutches under my arms, and slide off the table. We're on our way up to see Dr. Derby. He wants to see the braces.

"Ma, can we take the stairs?" I can't wait to try stairs.

"Yes, Ricky, but take your time. Let's not fall down the stairs the first time."

It's tiring and it feels funny. I can't believe it, we're in a building and I'm walking up the stairs almost like Mom. I can't wait to get into Dr. Derby's office and sit down. For the first time, I can sit without my legs sticking out. I can't wait to take the bus. I can sit in the seat and bend my knees. Wait till Bob and Fred see this!

Fourth grade is terrible. Mrs. Decker is so hard. She reminds me of Bob's description of the nuns at his school. Last year was so easy. I never got in trouble. Now I'm in trouble every day. I talk too much, I have so much trouble with spelling, and I never go out for recess. I have to stay in and do make up work almost every day. When I do get to go out for recess there's not much to do. One of the big kids in the other fourth grade class likes to pick on the small kids. He's not done anything to me, but he looks my way sometimes. He's a bully. He better think twice about bothering me!

It's the beginning of the day and we're saying the Pledge of Allegiance. I like to stand beside my desk with my right hand on my heart and say it, but the best part is the song after: "God Bless America." I have a favorite part in the song.

I look over at Cindy. She's the prettiest girl in the class. I wish I could talk with her, stand beside her, guide her. I think about her every time we sing it—she never notices me.

Mom and Dad say we're moving soon, but we're not moving far. Mom says she's going to have to get a job for us to move or else we're going to have to eat a lot more Spam again. I don't mind; I like Spam. Mom fries it in a pan, fries eggs, and puts an egg on top. We either have peas or string beans from a can with the Spam and egg. Now we have more meatloaf and chipped beef on toast. I wouldn't mind more Spam.

I'm in bed and Mom and Dad are talking. "I'll be going in at Stella's at 6:30 and if they have a banquet, I'll work Saturdays. This Saturday might be my first day. If not, I start Monday night."

"What time are you through?" Dad asks.

"When the kitchen's clean," Mom answers. "Probably about 11:30. Doris said she can pick me up and drop me off for a few dollars a week. I'll give them their bath and do Ricky's exercises before dinner and you'll just have to put them in bed."

Mom and Dad don't sound happy. I'm not happy; Mom won't be at home at night.

I hear Dad say, "We'll be moved in, in two weeks."

Mom says with a tired voice, "I can't wait, but we've got to get packing. Two weeks and we're moving! I hope there're kids near the house for Ricky and Donna to play with."

I know Dad's going to miss Mom at night. It's going to be different now.

Just before we moved, Mom worked on a Saturday and Dad works a half a day at Auto Gear, so our cousin Sandy watched Donna and me. Sandy drives a car, so she came in the morning to get me and Donna and we went to a pond near Sandy's house. A lot of Sandy's friends were there and a lot of them were boys. I think it's because Sandy's so pretty. They played the car radio while we swam in the pond. I can't walk good, but I can swim, as Mom says, like a fish. I like watching Sandy and her friends and listening to the music. My favorite song is "Blueberry Hill" by Fats Domino.

Sandy sang it all day. We went home late that afternoon and Dad wasn't home yet. Sandy had us get back in the car. She said, "I think I know where your father is. I heard him say he was going to see some friends after work."

We drove toward the center of town and started driving down the big hill near the stores. About half way down the hill, Sandy and I saw Dad's car slowly coming up the hill past us. Dad was looking straight ahead. He didn't even see us. Sandy stopped to buy some cigarettes and started back to the Project. When we got home, Dad was upstairs getting sick. He sounded so bad. Donna started to cry. I was scared too. I've never heard Dad get sick. After a while, Dad came downstairs. He looked sick and smelled like beer. He told Sandy he was okay and she could go. I didn't think Dad looked good. He sat down on the couch and held Donna, telling her everything was okay. She sat on Dad's lap with her head on his chest and her thumb in her mouth. Mom came home early that night. I listened for Mom and Dad to talk while I lay in bed, but I didn't hear anything. I knew Mom was mad, very mad.

CHAPTER 13

The Burning Bush

Our new house is a two family like the one Bob lives in but smaller. It's on the same street as the Project but on the other side of the street. It's the same distance as the Project from school on the south side of the school rather than the north. Donna and I have our own bedroom. Mom and Dad's bedroom is the living room. The dining room will be our living room. We live on the first floor and the landlord is on the second. They're old and the lady's not very friendly. The man is nice. The lady doesn't talk to us or even look at us. Mom says the lady only makes comments. One day she walked down the hallway by the front door and saw Mom and Dad's bedroom.

"Don't they know where the bedroom is?" she said. She wasn't even talking to anybody. I waited for Mom to say something, but she told Dad she bit her tongue. I hope it didn't hurt. I think Mom means she held her tongue; she didn't say anything.

"What's the matter, Dad?" I ask with concern. Dad looks so frustrated.

"I can't get the furnace to stay lit."

It's late. Mom's working, Donna's sick, and it's cold in the house.

"I'll be right back up."

Dad's gone downstairs into the cellar to try to get the fire started. We have a coal furnace and Dad said it's hard to keep it going.

He's never used a coal furnace. I'm on Mom and Dad's bed watching the late night movie. It ends and Dad's still downstairs. Mom will be home soon. The TV station is going off the air; the song they play sounds so lonely. I hear it a lot since we moved here. I wish Mom would come home.

Donna's been real sick for over a week now. She's been running a fever and coughing a lot. The doctor said she had to go into the hospital. Tonight's her first night there. This is different. Donna's only been in once before and she was with me. That's when we had pneumonia. I don't like not going with her; she's going to be scared. I'm at Aunt Ruth and Uncle Al's until Mom and Dad leave the hospital after visiting Donna.

Aunt Ruth and Uncle Al have moved to a bigger apartment in another part of the City. It's on the first floor of a two family home. No more walking up to their fourth floor apartment. Uncle Al's at work and Aunt Ruth and I are watching television. Mom and Dad should be here any time now. We're watching Wagon Train. I hope we get to watch the whole show; it's almost over.

As the show ends I hear someone coming in the kitchen door. It's Mom and Dad. Aunt Ruth and I get up and walk into the kitchen.

"Would you like a coffee?" Aunt Ruth asks.

Mom says yes, she never refuses a cup of coffee. Mom and Dad sit at the kitchen table.

Aunt Ruth asks, "What did the doctor say?"

Mom says in a soft, tired voice, "She's got rheumatic fever."

"Oh no," Aunt Ruth says as she slowly turns to Dad. I don't know if she's waiting for him to say something. Dad looks tired; he's rubbing his forehead with his palm.

Aunt Ruth asks, "Do you have a headache?"

"Yes," Dad says, "I've already taken some aspirin."

"Ma, what's rheumatic fever?"

Mom explains that it means Donna's very sick and it might affect her heart. I can see by the look on everyone's face that one question is enough.

⁓

Today's Sunday and Donna's coming home from the hospital. I'm at Aunt Ruth's again waiting. Uncle Al's home and getting ready for work. I'm kneeling on the couch looking out the window. They should be here any minute now. There's the car. Dad parks the car and Mom and Dad get out. Dad's carrying Donna. She looks much better. They come in the door and Dad puts Donna down. Uncle Al picks her up and gives her a hug. Mom told me Donna has a slight heart murmur and can't take dance lessons anymore. Maybe someday she can again. Dad still looks tired, but at least he's got a little smile. Aunt Ruth made a roast and everybody's hungry. It's been a long week.

⁓

Before Dad went to work today, he put the Christmas tree out at the street for trash, but the landlady didn't like it there. After Dad went to work, she decided to move it herself. She's a tall, thin, woman and the long black coat, black gloves, and her long gray hair made her seem evil. I was watching her out the window dragging the tree down the driveway to the back yard. Mom came over to watch.

"What's she doing?" Mom asks.

"I don't know. She went in the little shed in the back and came out with a big can."

Mom says mostly to herself, "What's she going to do with that gasoline? She's crazy," Mom chuckles. "Doesn't she know the tree's been treated?"

The landlady pours some gasoline on the tree, lights a match, and throws it at the tree. It's a cold windy day and she's standing so that the wind is at her back. Lucky because when the match touches the tree it explodes with fire. I can see the gasoline is burning, but not the tree.

Mom laughs and says, "That looks like Moses and the burning bush, but she's no Moses."

Mom says it's like a biblical moment. The landlady sets fire to the tree three times before it actually starts to burn. Sitting in the window watching her, I feel like I'm watching the forces of good and evil fighting and evil has all the power.

Two things happened that convinced Mom and Dad we had to move. One day Aunt Ruth and Uncle Al were visiting and Dad thought he heard a noise at the front door. He finally walked slowly and quietly to the door. Dad opened the door quickly and the landlady fell in the door. She said she was leaning on the door tying her shoes, but Mom and Dad didn't believe her. They said many times they thought she listened at the door. Mom and Dad were also unhappy that the landlady wasn't polite when she spoke to me. For Christmas that year I got a two wheel bike with training wheels. It was black with diamonds on it, saddle bags, and a place to put a rifle. I tried to ride it, but my left leg just wasn't strong enough.

One day when I was trying to ride the landlady said, "Why bother?"

Mom didn't bite her tongue this time. She came out of the house and said, "Don't you ever talk to my son again like that." The landlady just walked away.

I'm walking to school and I walk past Cindy's house. Her house is right behind the store across from the school. She never comes out when I walk by. Sometimes I walk down to her house just to see if she's outside. I've never seen her anyplace but in class. I'd like to stand here and wait to see if she comes out, but I think she'd just stay in the house. I can't say I remember her ever talking to me.

I get to class worried about a spelling test we had yesterday. I don't think I did very good. First thing after the Pledge of Allegiance and "God Bless America," Mrs. Decker hands back our tests. I got a 65.

Mrs. Decker walks to my desk and says, "Well, young man, I guess you're staying in today."

She's mad because I got a lot of words wrong and again I didn't spell Wednesday correctly. I do it all the time. I know it's not "Wendesday," but it looks right. It's the only day of the week I can't spell. When recess time arrives, I'm sitting in class writing Wednesday 100 times. Mrs. Decker's sitting at her desk writing.

At some point she looks up and calls my name. "Ricky, why don't you try to do better? Come up here."

I do try. I'm just as upset as she is. It's not easy studying after school. I'm tired by the time I get home from school. I get outta my seat and walk up to her desk.

Mrs. Decker says, "Come around here to my chair."

Mrs. Decker tells me I'm going to have a hard time if I don't work harder and then she picks me up onto her lap and just looks at me. Mrs. Decker doesn't say anything; she just looks and then I see a tear roll down her cheek. She wipes her cheek and looks away. I feel so bad. I know I made Mrs. Decker cry. That night I tell Mom I couldn't remember how to spell Wednesday. I didn't tell Mom I made Mrs. Decker cry.

Mom says, "It's easy, your father and I were married on a Wed-nes-day."

I wish Mom told me that a long time ago. Wed like wedding or to be wed! Now I get it, and I won't forget it.

It's the end of the school year and we're going to have graduation on Friday. With only four grades in this school, next year everyone's going to the new school. I'm not going; we're moving to the City. Mom wants to quit working and we can't stay in town if she quits. It costs too much. Dad will also be closer to work. We're having a big assembly at school Friday and all the parents are coming. We've been practicing the song "Catch a Falling Star" for weeks.

I don't really care if we move to the City. The only person I'll miss is Cindy. There's a good reason I'm ready to move. Yesterday I was out playing in the field next to the house next door. I was there with Francis who lives in the house next door, and Tommy, who lives on the other side of the field. We were looking for grass hoppers when Francis' little sister, Gail, came out into the field. She's Donna's friend. I noticed she was whispering to Francis and Tommy. The next thing I knew Tommy tackled me and he and Francis jumped on me and tried to hold me down. Gail stood nearby with a big smile on her face and I knew she was going to do something. I struggled to get away, but I couldn't get completely out from under them. I didn't want to hurt them and trying to get away, I got too tired to fight anymore. Both of them were sitting on my arms and Francis was holding my head. I knew then what was coming. Gail knelt down beside my head and kissed me on the mouth. It was terrible—she's just a little girl! I'm glad we're moving. I'd never hear the end of it next year in school.

I hope Dad and I continue to play catch when we move to the City. When we moved here, Uncle Al bought me a baseball glove and a hard ball. It's a good one, real leather. It looks like a professional glove. Dad and I have been playing catch all spring at least two or three times a week. I love spending the time with Dad, but he throws the ball hard. I'm a good catch, but then I have to be. Dad throws so hard I'm afraid not to catch the ball. It stings the palm of my hand when I catch it.

Dad says if it stings then I'm catching it right. I thought Dad would slow the pitch down when I told him, but he didn't. He seems so serious when he pitches. I sometimes wonder how he feels about me not being able to do what the other boys do. Dad likes the New York Yankees and he loves it when Mickey Mantle comes to the plate. A lot of the other boys play little league and I know Dad would like me to be able to play, but I'm not going to be on a team. I can play when it's with a few friends or with Uncle Jerry and Fred but not a real team.

No slow pitches for me. Dad wants me to be tough. I catch the fast ones just like all the other boys. I can be afraid of the pitches and still not stop; I like the time with my Dad.

CHAPTER 14

Ware?

~⁓

We've moved to the City and we're living in a bigger house. It's a two family like the one we were living in, but it's bigger like Bob's. It's old; I know because there's an ice box on the wall right next to the back door. There's a little door on the outside that Dad said the ice man would open to deliver ice, but we don't need an ice man because we have a refrigerator. Actually, I don't know anyone who has an ice man now. On the inside of the house there's a small door into the icebox where you would keep food that has to stay cold. There's not a lot of room in the icebox so I guess in the olden days people didn't have much food that had to stay cold.

When we were in the Project, we had a milk man and bread man, but we haven't had them stop at our house since we left the Project. I'm glad we don't have the bread man anymore because he carried a great big wire basket filled with donuts, pastry and bread. Mom always said we can't afford the donuts and pastry. We don't have a bread man anymore, but I can still smell the donuts and pastry. I don't think I'll ever forget the sweet smell that the bread man left behind in our kitchen at the Project.

There's a park across the street from our house and it's full of kids today. I can see swings and seesaws and a baseball field. Maybe tomorrow I'll walk over and check it out. The school I'm going to is four blocks away. It's old too and across the street from the school is a hospital, the City Hospital. Mom says Donna and I were born there. I hear people in the park speaking a different language and they look different; their skin is dark but not as dark as John's. They live on the street one block away. Mom says they're from Puerto Rico.

In this house, Donna and I have our own bedrooms and we have a pantry for food. All the rooms are big and airy with big windows and high ceilings. This house looks bigger than all the others around. All the houses are two family with big porches, but this house is the biggest. There's a lot of fancy wood around the doors and windows, and wood floors. The house is great, but there's something else I really like about living here. On the other side of the park there's a little store that sells penny candy. I'm going to start getting an allowance because I'm washing the dishes every night after supper. Now I'll have money to buy candy. Mom says I can only spend a nickel every week for candy but that's five pieces. I've never had five pieces of candy at the same time.

Donna starts first grade this year in our new school. The best part is that we're going to the same school. If we stayed in town, Donna and I would have been in different schools. Well maybe not. Mom says they were thinking of keeping me back in fourth grade if we stayed in Town, but now I am going to fifth grade. Mom says they're a year behind here so I'm not going to stay back. Anyway, I like having Donna nearby when Mom's not around. I can make sure she's alright at lunch and recess.

With us moving here, one other thing is changing. We're going to go to another church. In Town we used to go to a little old, white church with a tall steeple. The best part of going to this church is that we're going to the same church Fred and Little Leota go to. Mom said she went to this church when she was a little girl. I guess this church is old too.

Oh yes … Wednesday, Wally said I could stop wearing the half brace. She said she talked to Dr. Derby and he said okay. Thursday we went and got a new heel on my left shoe because of the hole through the heel that my brace attaches to. Now I have no brace on the left leg. It's still not very strong, but I can walk a little bit around the house with just one crutch. I use one crutch under my right arm.

People are always asking if the crutches hurt and wonder why I don't have padding. They don't hurt and I don't need padding. Maybe when you're bigger they hurt. I've tried the padding on the top of my crutch and it feels like a big hot dog bun under my arm. It looks like a big hot dog bun. I don't need the padding for the part I hold onto either. I've got callouses on all the places that touch the crutch: my palms, the knuckle on my thumbs, the middle knuckle on my first finger, and where my wrist touches the crutch. I'd rather have callouses than the padding.

Today I'm at the park across the street and I've met a boy my age. I told him I just moved here and he said he and his family moved here a few years ago.

"Where did you move from?" I ask.

"Ware."

"Yes, where?" I ask again.

The boy smiles and says, "We moved here from Ware."

He didn't say it like he was asking me a question. I'll try again. "Yes, that's what I said, where?"

"Ware," he says again.

I'm so confused. I'm lost in this conversation. I don't know what to say next. Suddenly the boy begins to laugh and I don't know if he's making fun of me or not.

"I'm sorry; this happens a lot."

I'm no less confused, but I'm feeling more comfortable he isn't making fun of me.

"I used to live in a town that's named Ware; it's spelled w-a-r-e. Whenever I get asked where I'm from, this happens."

We both sit down on a bench and talk, my first new friend in the City. His name is Larry.

CHAPTER 15

The Other Camp

~

All summer long I've been waiting for this. Today I'm going to summer camp. It's a long drive up into the Taconic Mountains. We pulled off the main road a little while ago and now we're on a rough road. We're way out in the woods. I see a field ahead; it looks like we've arrived. There's a big American flag on the field and a large building at the right rear corner. To the left of the field is a row of cabins and beyond the field is a large lake. Not so big you can't see the other side but larger than any other lake I've ever seen. I see a long dock with canoes and row boats. We all climb out of the car and step into the sun. Donna looks nervous. Dad noticed; he's picking her up.

Suddenly I hear someone speaking loud like they're talking through a bull horn; they're telling us to come to the center of the field. Yes, there's a man standing on a small platform and he is speaking through a bull horn. As everyone walks toward the field, I see there are a lot of people here.

"Hello campers and your families. Welcome to Camp Taconic. I'm Mr. Roberts, the leader here at Camp Taconic. You boys can call me Mr. R."

Mr. Roberts goes on and introduces us to his staff of counselors and tells us the rules of the camp. The counselors are walking to the cabins while Mr. Roberts continues. He's describing our typical daily activities. I like this: swimming, boating, hiking, and eating. He says that the eating's the best part because we've got the best cook in all the camps in the USA. The cook's name is Mr. Thomson and we can call him Mr. T. Now Mr. Roberts is calling out our names and our cabin assignments. He says we can go to our cabins when we get our number. After some time we hear that I'm in cabin number five. Our parents have to go get out suitcases and meet us at our cabin.

It looks like there're 10 cabins. They all look the same except for the numbers over the door. There're four bunks in the cabin. Soon four boys, their parents, and a few younger brothers and sisters are standing in the cabin. I think I know who the four campers are. One is tall and looks a little tough, another is even taller and heavy, and the last guy is just a little taller than me and skinny as a rail. The counselor steps in the door and introduces himself.

"Hi boys, brothers and sisters, and moms and dads; my name is Tony Morris."

The tough looking boy only has his mom with him.

"I have badges here with each of your names on them. When I call your name raise your hand."

The first name he calls is Paul. That's the skinny kid. The next is Alan. He's the tall, heavy kid. Next he calls me then the tough looking kid, Chris.

"Okay boys, say hi to each other and shake hands."

It's confusing, but we finally all shake hands. I notice that Alan has wet hands, probably from sweating outside. Chris has a limp handshake, not what I expected. Dad says we should always give a firm handshake. I like to give a firm handshake, but my little hand gets lost in some of the adults hands. Next, Tony assigns us to our beds, he calls them bunks, and tells us what he expects of us in the cabin such as making our bunks every morning and keeping our area clean. After listening to Mr. Roberts and Tony, it's apparent that no foolishness is going to be tolerated. We have to stick to a tight schedule every day and the schedule's full. The camp and cabin rules are posted on the wall and tomorrow's schedule is on our bunk.

Tony continues. "Time to make up your bunks. This is the last time this week your mothers will help you make your bed. From now on you're responsible. After you're done with that, it's time for the moms and dads to say goodbye and then I want you to sit on your bunk. Make sure your suitcase is under your bunk after you make it up."

Mom and I make my bunk and Dad talks with Tony. We finish with the bunk, put the suitcase under, and say our goodbyes. I sit on my bunk and wait for the other parents to leave. Now it's just Tony and the four of us. Tony tells us we're going take a tour of the camp, return to our cabin, and when the dinner bell rings, eat dinner. He also tells us about the morning routine; wake up at 7 o'clock to revelry, dress, clean our area, make our beds, line up for breakfast, and march to the mess hall. He used the term march. Sounds like Cub Scouts.

Tomorrow we're starting out at archery, then a short hike followed by lunch. After lunch we rest for an hour on our bunks and then go to the lake for swimming and boating lessons. Next we prepare for dinner and march to the mess hall to eat. Preparing for dinner means going back to the cabin, changing out of our swim trunks, and lining up outside the cabin. When we finish dinner we'll play a game on the field and end the day around a campfire. The day ends at 9 p.m. To me it sounds like I've died and gone to heaven, a full week hanging out with the guys doing guy things. Tony walks to the door and tells us to fall in. He says that means to line up behind him according to height, the shortest first. That puts me right behind Tony.

We take our tour and return to our cabin. Tony says we have about a half an hour before the dinner bell, so spend some time getting to know each other. Tony leaves and we slowly start to ask questions. It doesn't take long for us to learn that we're all 10 years old. Three of us are going into the fifth grade. Chris stayed back last year so he's staying in the fourth grade. He said he hangs out with kids in junior high and considering his height I'm not surprised. I can't imagine him in the fourth grade. Chris and I live in a city but not the same city. Paul and Alan live in small towns. Paul seems okay. His bunk is on the same side of the cabin as mine. We sleep head to head against the outside wall. The cabin is just one room so we're all together with little privacy. Not a big deal for four boys. The counselors have their own cabins. They're guards who patrol the area at night to make sure nobody gets in trouble. Tony says we'll never even know the guards are there. Alan is real homesick. He's been looking sadder and sadder since his mom and dad left. The rest of us could care less.

Chris picks this time to share something that I think he believes will, as Mom says, move him up the pecking order.

It starts with, "Hey, any of you guys ever kissed a girl?"

What do I say? I'm not going to tell them about Gail. We don't kiss in my family and certainly no girl that I'm willing to admit to has ever kissed me. Is there something I don't know that happens when a boy and girl kiss that Chris could catch me at if I lie? I guess I better be truthful. As I expected, Paul, Alan, and I all say no. I was really hoping to have something about girls to share, but I've got nothing. On the pecking order, Paul, Alan and I are tied for dead last!

The truth be told Chris didn't have much for details. For the moment, Alan's mood has improved. I'm feeling a little bit confused. I'm interested in whatever sketchy details Chris is offering about kissing a girl, but I haven't a clue what he's talking about. Paul's asking for more details, but the dinner bell rings and Tony's waiting for us outside the cabin. When we're assembled and quiet, our counselors march us to the mess hall. Kissing a girl … I hope I don't have to wait too long before that happens. I know I'm curious—very curious.

After dinner we learn how to play "Steal the Flag." It's a lot of running and the guys seem a little worried about my crutches. A few guys tried to get the towel out of my belt to send me to jail, but all I had to do was move a crutch near them and they backed off. I'm too slow to catch anybody, but I have a great time trying. After the game we sit around a campfire and the counselors lead us in song; one of them plays the guitar. It's fun, but I can see that we're all tired. I'm ready to get to bed. Finally, we're in our bunks and taps is playing. After a few minutes I hear Alan softly crying. The big kid crying, it's like the first day of school all over again.

Eating in the mess hall is without a doubt better than I could ever imagine. I'm always hungry and we can eat as much as we want. I don't know if it's our hunger or the cook, Mr. T, but the food's the best I've ever tasted. We've had eggs, bacon, sausage, pancakes, syrup, hamburgs, hot dogs, chicken, ham, hash, fruit, cake, ice cream, and pie and it's only Tuesday. Today in swim safety, we learned how to survive if we we're stranded in the water far from shore. You take off your pants, tie the bottom of each leg into a knot, pull up the zipper, and snap the button. Then you put your pants behind you holding onto a belt loop in each hand. Next, you pull your pants quickly over your head. The legs fill with air and your pants float. You can rest in the crotch of the pants for five minutes before you have to fill the pants with air again. It all looked so easy when our swimming instructor showed us on the dock.

The swim instructor tells us to put our jeans on over our suits and get in the water, no jumping. It was easy to get my jeans off even though I was underwater the whole time. You can't tread water while you're taking off your pants. I've got so I can tread water a little by moving my left leg from side to side. Now I have to tie a knot in the pant legs. Sounds easy enough, but we're in water over our heads and my method of treading water with my leg isn't all that effective. I can stay afloat all day if I can use my arms. I finally discover that if I float on my back I can get it done. When I finish tying the knots, I pull my jeans over my head and sure enough they fill with air. It's not easy because wet jeans are heavy, but I get it done. It works! We all float around satisfied with ourselves. Well, most of us. A few of the guys probably can't even tie their shoes because they can't tie a knot in the legs of their jeans.

⁓

It's Friday morning and Tony tells us that we're going to visit another camp. On our daily schedule it says outing. Since our arrival at camp we've all believed that there's a girl's camp on the other side of the lake. Every night after the first night in our cabin, we've talked about girls. We've spent a lot of time thinking about a way to get across that lake without being caught and now they're going to take us there by bus. We're sure the other camp is a girl's camp. We talk about it all through breakfast. We work hard containing our excitement. We don't want Tony to see how excited we are. When we finish breakfast, Tony reminds us to go brush our teeth and line up outside the cabin. We move like cheetahs. When we get back to the cabin, the buses are lined up waiting to take us to the girl's camp. We get on the buses and no one says a word. There is nothing more to talk about—this is it.

After riding for 15 minutes or so the buses pull into a camp and immediately I notice there aren't any girls running around. In the distance we see a large group of kids near a group of buildings. I notice a boy in a wheelchair, then another. There is even a couple of kids with crutches. Some of the boys are walking but with difficulty. Their legs and arms seem to move erratically. I get off the bus and the kids in the camp look at me—they're all staring at me.

Finally, one of the boys walks up to me and says, "What are you doing with them?"

For a moment, I don't know what he means and then I realize.

All I can think to say is, "Why aren't you with us?"

I've never seen a group of handicapped kids together. I can't understand why we aren't all together. We stay at the camp for a couple of hours talking with the kids and playing board games. It's fun, but I feel uneasy the whole time. Why would adults want to keep us separate?

Tonight is our last night at camp. Around the campfire everyone is very sad. We sing and do skits we prepared all week. The best skit is done by the guys in cabin nine. They dress like they're in the military and three of the guys are running around searching for the very important papers. Finding the papers is a matter of national security. Finally, the fourth guy runs on to the little stage with a roll of toilet paper saying he found the very important papers. The other three grab the roll of toilet paper and run off the stage. We're laughing so hard. It seems that all the talk here in camp is about bodily functions or girls. I don't ever remember joking about bodily functions with Bob or Fred.

It was a great time, but when it's over, we all go back to our bunks sad that the week is over.

Saturday morning we pack up and our parents start arriving. Mom and Dad arrive and tell me we're going to Fred's. It relieves some of the sadness of the moment. We say our goodbyes and we're off.

I can't help asking, "Ma did you know there's a camp nearby with all handicapped kids? Why are they alone?"

CHAPTER 16

Poor Little Fool

~)

When we get to Fred's, he's outside waiting for me with the red wagon. We've been using the red wagon to get around the neighborhood for years now. Fred pushes and I steer. We don't use it all the time. When we do, it's for a special reason.

Where're we going, Fred, to the hill?" I ask as I get out of the car.

"Absolutely," Fred says.

The hill is behind the school on the next block. Riding down the hill is not the best part; the best part is when we get half way down and turn the handle. The wagon turns and tips over. We roll down the hill with the wagon chasing us. It's so exciting. It's dangerous and we like a little danger. We discovered this by accident one day.

We were coming through the field behind the school and we went near the hill. I said we should ride down the hill and Fred pushed me to the edge. I started down and half way down one of the front wheels hit a rock, the handle turned, and I rolled down the hill. It was great. Next Fred tried it and he liked it too, so we've been doing it ever since with just one change since the first time—I leave the crutches at the top of the hill.

"Oh! Fred, I almost forgot to show you, look no brace." I stick out my left leg and lift my pant leg to show him.

"Wow! How does it feel?"

"It feels light!"

We spend a few hours making runs down the hill until we're ready to move on. There's more to do.

"Hey, Fred, let's go look for some bottles."

I don't know why I bother to suggest this idear. We've never found a discarded bottle, but just the possibility makes it worthwhile. The return from one bottle means a couple of pieces of candy each because Fred's got a store with penny candy near his house too.

"Okay," Fred says.

This time I don't ride in the wagon. We're always so sure we're going to find a bunch of bottles. We're going to need an empty wagon for all the bottles we're going to find. Besides, I have to be walking to look for bottles. We look behind every store on Park Street, the main road near Fred's house, and along the road. Finally we give up. It was fun, but as usual we're unsuccessful. Someday we'll find a bunch of bottles—someday.

"It's got to be near time for dinner," I tell Fred.

Fred smiles and says, "Yeah, let's get home."

We both know what the smile means; after dinner we get to burn the trash. I've never lived in a house where you can burn trash in the backyard, but they do at Fred's. Fred and I make believe that cartons are buildings. I hope there're lots of cartons tonight. Mom says we're going to be a couple of pyros someday.

When we get home, dinner's not ready, so Fred and I head upstairs to his room to play our favorite imagination game, space ship. Fred's room is big; there're two beds and other furniture in the room and there's still almost as much space as my entire room. It's a great place to make believe we're in a space ship. We travel all over the universe visiting strange planets inhabited by horrible beasts. The windows in the room are our portals to danger and victory. Like our battles on the way home from the movies, we always win.

Fred has to share the room with his little brother, Paul, but Paul's not like Bob's brother, Stevie. Paul doesn't bother us when we're in the room. I'm not saying Paul's not a pain, it's just he seems to know better when Fred and I are playing in the room. Aunt Leota calls Fred downstairs to put the wagon in the cellar, so I start to set up the control panel for the space ship. It's made up of the boards from Chutes and Ladders and Sorry and has Checkers pieces as knobs. It was while I was setting it up that it happened. I started to think about what my Dad and Uncle Windy have for toys and I realized men don't play with toys. I started to get this powerful feeling that I can only describe as fear. I started to sweat and shake. Just the thought of not being able to play with toys scared me so much. It took me a few minutes to calm down, I'm gonna try to not think about that again.

Fred no more than gets back to the room and Mom calls us to dinner. On the way down the stairs Fred says, "Hey, Rick, let's ask if you can stay over tonight." The answer to our question is yes. Now that's a surprise. Our moms barely ever say yes. It's only yes if it's their idear. Tomorrow's Sunday and Monday is Labor Day, so to our surprise our moms say yes to two nights. This is better than finding bottles. Tomorrow we have Sunday school; Aunt Net's our Sunday school teacher. Considering that we're supposed to sit quietly for an hour while Aunt Net talks, we have a lot of fun, at least Fred and I have a lot of fun. Everything's so funny when we're together. We sit around a big table and Fred sits across from me on the other end of the table from Aunt Net. Fred makes faces. He can screw up his face and put it back before anyone sees him. Then he plays so serious.

It's hard not to laugh out loud. I have to make believe I'm picking something up under the table and hold my hand over my mouth. Aunt Net is Nana's sister, so we should know better, but we can't stop. We've got to be careful not to make Aunt Net too mad because she could turn us in to our moms. I know Fred's going to get us in trouble someday.

Today's Monday and Mom's whole family gets together for the family Labor Day picnic at Mitny Park. It's always been a great time. We get to play badminton and we get to tease the younger cousins.

The best thing is Fred and I put dry ice in the drinking fountain. It makes the water in the fountain look like its boiling and the younger kids won't go near the fountain. I wonder if they'll ever figure it out.

Each year we end the day with a baseball game. Fred and I are always on the winning team because we're on Uncle Jerry and my Dad's team. Uncle Jerry is Mom's youngest brother. He goes to college and plays football. I get to bat; someone else runs for me. I also play the outfield. There're four of us in the outfield, so it doesn't matter that I can't chase the ball. If it comes right to me, I get it.

This might be the best day of the summer even if it's the end of summer. We just got home from the picnic; it's late afternoon and I'm sitting on the back porch. The porch faces the street that leads to the school. I'm looking down the street thinking about tomorrow morning and school, when I see a mom and dad come out of a house a couple of houses down on the other side with two girls and a little boy. They all get into the car in front of the house and then it happens.

A girl, a beautiful girl, with long brown hair comes running out of the house, down the steps, and jumps into the car. The graceful, effortless way she runs, her hair sailing behind her, and her dress billowing as she runs down the stairs to the car—what a sight! Does she go to my school? I can't wait for tomorrow morning.

We're all ready for school and walking with Mom. Mom's taking Donna for her first day of school. I'm walking ahead because there's no way I want other kids to think I'm with my Mother. I know where my classroom is and I'm headed for it. Here's the house I saw that girl come out of yesterday. I wish she came out before I got here. Of course, maybe she doesn't go to my school.

"Hi."

Who said that?

"Hello." Mom answers.

I turn my head and see it's the woman I saw yesterday come out of the house where the girl lives; she said hi to Mom. There she is, the girl, and here I am ahead of Mom and Donna. Boy it never works out. Mom and the woman are talking.

Oh no, Mom's looking at me. "Ricky, come and meet Mrs. Segal and her daughters." Okay, put on a smile.

"This is my son Ricky. This is Mrs. Segal, Rita, Cathy, and Mary Anne."

I say hi. Her name's Mary Anne. She's more beautiful up close and what a smile!

"Ricky's going to fifth grade and today is Donna's first day," Mom tells Mrs. Segal.

I can't stop looking at Mary Anne. She's got the cutest little nose and big brown eyes. Unfortunately, she's not looking at me; she's looking across the street. I look and see what's drawing her attention. There's a boy walking down the driveway at the house across the street. He's walking in the other direction. He probably goes to the junior high. He looks over at Mary Anne and she waves, but he looks away. She's still watching him like she expects him to wave back.

"So its Cathy's first day too," Mom says to Mrs. Segal.

"And Rita's in fourth and Mary Anne's in fifth," Mrs. Segal continues.

Mary Anne's in fifth; in my class? Could it be?

"Ricky's got Mrs. Jackson," Mom says.

"That's too bad; Mary Anne is in Mr. Theodore's class," Mrs. Segal says.

Figures!

"Shall we go?" Mrs. Segal suggests.

They all walk by me. I'm still watching the boy across the street. He doesn't look back; he ignored Mary Anne.

"Come on, Ricky," Mom says.

This isn't working out to be a good day. That song, "Poor Little Fool"; it's playing in my head.

Mary Anne's ignoring me just like the boy is ignoring her. Yeah, not a good day; poor little fool.

CHAPTER 17

Pen and Ink

My classroom is on the first floor, but at this school it means walking up a flight of stairs unless I walk around the building and go in the front door. Without the brace on my left leg, getting up and down the stairs is much easier. So I take the stairs. My first day and I see Larry walking into the school.

"Hey, Larry."

"Hi, Rick, who's your teacher?"

"I've got Mrs. Jackson."

"Too bad, I've got Mr. Theodore."

Sure he does; he's got Mary Anne in his class.

The classroom is big with a high ceiling and giant windows on one wall to my left. The windows face the street and I'm in the center of the row on the window side of the room. There're cars passing and I like to look out the window; it's easy to get lost in my thoughts. For now, my thoughts are on Mary Anne.

I've got so that I can get up and down the stairs without thinking about it. When I go upstairs, I put my left foot up on the next stair, lean forward a little, and with a little shove from my shoulders, arms and flick of my wrists I'm up on the next step. For a moment my left leg is all that's holding me up, but it has enough strength now that it will hold me until my crutches and right leg are on the stair. The fun part is when the distance from one stair to the next is greater than normal. That takes a little extra push and I have too much speed to easily stop my forward motion. Then I have to hit my crutches against the edge of the next stair to stop myself from falling forward.

Coming down the stairs takes a little more confidence because I lean forward and put my crutch tips down on the next step. Next I use my arms and shoulders to lift my weight off of my right leg and let it swing forward. Once the foot has cleared the step, I lower my right leg down to the next step and the left leg follows. I can only take one step at a time, but I can do it fast enough to not fall too far behind when I'm going up or down one flight.

Fifth grade has turned out to be a lot of fun. The work in class is so easy. The first time we had to write, I wrote in cursive, but most of the kids are still printing. For the first time, I feel like the smart one. This is going to be a good year. Good penmanship automatically makes you seem smarter and penmanship was a big deal in Town. There was one big surprise, something I've never seen before. We have ink wells in our desks and we're going to get ink to put in them today. What I can't imagine is what we would use for pens, feathers maybe?

After lunch we get our ink and ink pens. Mrs. Jackson spends too much time explaining all the things we can't do with the ink and the ink pens. I'm not sure it was a good idear because some of the things would have never crossed my mind. Finally, Mrs. Jackson hands out the pens. Personally, I'm disappointed. They're just black wood shafts that start out skinny at the top and taper out to a metal end that flares out from the wood to a point at the end. The metal end is shaped like an arrow head. It's split in half from the point up to a small hole near the part of the metal end that sticks into the wood shaft. Now the ink. It's black and in a bottle that goes in the well. I can see where this liquid could be dangerous.

It takes some time, but I've finally got the knack of writing with the ink pen. I've decided that playing around with the ink isn't cool, but target practice with the pen is okay. Not at my fellow students or Mrs. Jackson. The floors are made of long, thin wood boards. There're spaces between the boards, which make great targets for the pen. I can sit at my desk and aim for the space between the boards. I lean over toward the windows just a little and hold the end of the pen between my thumb and finger, close my left eye, and aim down the shaft for one of the spaces. Then I gently let go. If I hit it right, the pen sticks in the space between the boards standing straight up. The far left side of the room is a safe place out of Mrs. Jackson's view.

My grades are good because I already did a lot of the work last year, but there is one thing we do here that I've never done before. We square dance. Mrs. Jackson loves square dancing and she says we're going to love it too. I actually like it. I use one crutch and hold the girls with the other arm. The girls are so soft and smell so good. We can square dance all day as far as I'm concerned. I like to dance with Suzy from Atwater Terrace. That's an area up on the hill next to the hospital. Doctors live up there. You can't see the houses up on the hill with all the trees. Going up there is like going to another world. There are lots of trees and space between the houses. All the houses are a long ways from the road. The space is covered with grass. You could put a lot of houses like mine up there.

I was at Atwater Terrace because I was invited to a birthday party for Suzy. I was the only boy from my class there. The other boys were her cousins and her brother. Suzy's house has just one floor and only one family lives in it. No other apartments are connected to it. The stove and refrigerator in Suzy's house are shiny metal. Not white like ours. Her house is so big with rugs that go all the way to the wall. They look like they go under the wall. Even on a hot day like the day of Suzy's birthday, it was cool in her house. I'd love to live in her house.

It's October and some days are hot. Today's a warm day and Mrs. Jackson has the windows open. It's hard to think on a day like this.

The warm breeze, the rustling of the leaves...

"Ricky, did you hear me?" Mrs. Jackson startles me. What did she say?

"Mrs. Jackson, I'm sorry."

"I didn't think so."

The bell rings; I'm saved.

"Hold it, class, I haven't dismissed you." Maybe I'm not saved.

"Ricky, the class will leave and you can stay and write the answer to the question I asked 10 times on the board for the class to see tomorrow. You wouldn't want them to get this question wrong on a test would you, Ricky?"

I shake my head no.

"Okay, everyone except Ricky is excused."

Everyone jumps out of their seat.

Timmy, who sits in front of me, whispers as he stands up, "The date the Thirteenth Amendment was enacted."

I whisper back, "Thank you."

With everyone rushing out the door I stand up and go to the board and start to write; I want to try to catch up to everybody. Maybe I'll see Mary Anne.

Mrs. Jackson says, "So you do know the question?"

"Yes," I reply too quickly.

"Who told you?"

I'm trapped—I'm speechless—I don't want to get Timmy in trouble. I stand there with my mouth hanging open.

Luck is with me, Mrs. Jackson doesn't pursue her line of questioning. She says, "Okay, Ricky, write the answer and you're excused; pay attention in the future."

That was close. "I will, Mrs. Jackson."

I write December 18, 1865 on the board 10 times and run out of the room as fast as I can. I get to the stairs in a hurry. Maybe I can catch up. At the second step from the bottom, I lose my footing and catapult myself to the landing. This is the first time I've fallen down stairs. I'm shocked. My zipper tab must have been sticking out because it stuck into my groin. The air's knocked outta me and I feel this intense pain where the tab stuck into me. Then I hear the noise.

All I want to do is lie here for a moment and recover from this pain, but there, at the top of the steps, is Mr. Theodore and some of his students. Mr. Theodore's coming down the stairs with a worried look on his face. No way, I don't need any help. I've got to get up fast. Mr. Theodore's trying to help. I don't need any help.

"I'm okay," I tell him and run out the door.

Was Mary Anne one of the students? I hope she didn't see me on the floor. I don't like looking helpless. If I'm going to be a man, I have to be tough. Oh, that zipper hurt!

CHAPTER 18

A Teacher

~⁓

I got a Valentine's card in the mail today from Suzy. She told me to watch for something in the mail when I left school Thursday. It isn't one of those little cards. It's regular size. She must have bought it special for me. Yesterday was Lincoln's Birthday; I had to wait until today, Saturday. I can't believe it; a girl has never sent me anything before. Mom says I have to call and thank her. Call her? My hand's shaking so much holding the phone I'm not sure I can hold it to my ear. Well here goes. It's ringing.

I hear Suzy say hello. "Hi, Suzy, thank you for the Valentine's card." I say it so fast I'm not sure Suzy got it all.

I talk and talk and talk. I can't shut up; I'm afraid to let her talk.

After I get off the phone I'm angrier with myself than I've ever been. I know I sounded like a braggart; I couldn't help myself. I sounded like I think I'm the smartest kid in the class, well maybe I am, but I didn't need to sound that way. I also talked about my many travels to the ocean. I've been to the beach once. She's going to think I'm a fool. How stupid was that! Next year Suzy's going to a private school; I wish she would stay, so I can show her I'm not a jerk. Well, I've got the rest of the year. It was nice getting the card but why me? She's so much different than the rest of us. I don't understand why she pays special attention to me.

It's hard when people pay special attention, especially a girl like Suzy. Does she like me? Does she want to be my girlfriend? Or, is it something else? I don't even want to think about that possibility. Mom says people think I'm special because I am special, but why should I be special? I just had polio. That doesn't make me different or special. Mom says God treats some of us different because He has something important he needs us to do. He's willing to make life more difficult to prepare us. She says it's no different than how she treats me about exercise. She knows it hurts, but it prepares me for the future. If that's true, maybe this is all worthwhile. I guess I'll find out someday.

It would be so much easier to be like everybody else, not because I don't like walking on crutches. I want to be like everybody else, so that I know that someone like Suzy likes me for me. I don't know, maybe that's selfish.

It's been almost a week since I got Suzy's card. She smiled at me Monday, but I still feel like such a jerk bragging like I did. Well, actually it wasn't bragging, it was stretching the truth—really stretching. I wish I could apologize, but I'd probably make a bigger jerk outta myself. She seems so much older than the rest of us. I'm going to miss her next year. I wish I had more time to find out why she seems to like me.

It was a hard day today; I'm tired. God, I could use a miracle here. I need more energy. I'm tired, but I can't fall asleep, nothing new with that. Wally gave me a cane to practice with. It's cool. I can't walk very far yet with the cane, certainly not far enough to get to school, but it's a start. Dr. Derby wants to operate on my right foot this summer. I'm not sure I like that. You can die during an operation, and it's not going to make it easier to walk with the cane. I have to add walking with the cane to my exercises and that includes walking up and down stairs with the cane. Pretty soon I might not need the crutches at all.

I'm tired. Mom and Dad are watching television. I can hear Tennessee Ernie Ford talking. I hope he sings "Sixteen Tons." Yes, he is.

I love that song … it reminds me of doing my exercises; especially when he says a man is made outta muscle and blood.

I must have fallen asleep to "Sixteen Tons." I dreamt about the building again last night. I must have seen that building when I was very young, I don't remember ever seeing it. I hate the feeling, loneliness—overwhelming loneliness. If the building exists, I wonder what happened there. I get down outta bed and walk on my knees to the kitchen. What's that ticking noise?

"Ma, do you hear a ticking noise?"

"No, after you eat breakfast and get your brace on, I want you to vacuum your room and practice with the cane."

Mom says it with the same rush she always uses on Saturday morning. I don't like Saturdays. Dad's at work and Donna and I help with the cleaning. I don't mind work, but I don't like cleaning. You no more than finish and things start getting dirty again.

"Oh, here's what's making the ticking, I've got a tack stuck in my knee."

"Oh my goodness, does it hurt?" Mom asks as she steps over to look.

"No," I reply as I pull out the tack. Pulling it out hurts a little. "Someone must have dropped the tack and I put my knee on it."

That gnawing noise is keeping me awake tonight. Dad said it's probably rats. Mom is so mad; she's ready to move. Our landlord is a rabbi and Dad said he prepares chickens in the cellar; actually I think he said the rabbi kills them in the cellar. I've never heard any chickens. Dad said if a rabbi prepares the chickens it makes them kosher. I have no idear what that means. The rabbi said he would get rid of the rats, but it sounds like the rats are going to eat the house before the rabbi gets a chance to do anything. This afternoon I went in the pantry and opened a cupboard and there it was—a rat as big as a small cat! Hey that rhymes. He was gone before I could move. My mistake was yelling rat. Mom went crazy. She likes a very clean house and that was too much for her. Mom emptied all the food out of the pantry and put everything on tables in the kitchen. I don't think that'll stop the rats.

My mind wanders to Mary Anne. I wonder how I can get her to notice me. She seems to only pay attention to the older boy who lives across from her and he acts like she's not even alive. What's wrong with girls? They always seem to want what they can't have. I know what I could do. I could have a play and I could be the father and Mary Anne could be the mother. She can't help but get to know me. I'll write the play and ask Mary Anne to be in it.

I've got to come up with more than just who will be what in the play. I'm not having much luck. This isn't as easy as I thought. I'm tired. Maybe I better ask Mom for help. Friday Mom and I go to Our Lady for a meeting with Dr. Derby and some other doctors. They will tell Dr. Derby if he can do the surgery. Dr. Derby says it's just a formality in my case. Mom and I are going because the doctors want to talk to me. I'll ask Mom Friday about writing the play with me. Okay, now I've got to get to sleep; my mind won't stop.

Walking to the hospital, we stopped at Aunt Ruth's and Mom had a coffee. I think that's why we stopped. Mom loves coffee. I can't wait until I can drink coffee. I drink tea when I stay at Aunt Rita's, but Mom says I'm still too young for coffee. The hospital is old. It's a Catholic hospital and there're nuns here. I wonder if they're like Bob's teacher. It smells the same as the Weston Hospital. Here comes Dr. Derby.

"Hi, Henri, and how's Ricky doing today."

"I'm doing great, Dr. Derby."

"That's what I like to hear; you always have a smile. Let's go in here and sit down and I'll explain what's going to happen this morning. The other doctors will be here in a few minutes."

Dr. Derby opens the door next to us, and we walk into a big room with a high ceiling and big windows at the other end of the room that only allow a little light in. The windows have long drapes and what Mom calls shears. We have shears on our windows.

There's a long table with big chairs around it in front of the windows. Where we walked in, there're a lot of chairs in rows with a center aisle. Dr. Derby turns on the lights and we walk down the aisle and sit in the front.

"Now, what we're here for is to describe to the other doctors why I think this surgery is necessary. It's only a formality as I said, but it's necessary. In cases like this, the doctors like to meet the patient. Ricky, they will ask you a few questions. Just answer their questions as best you can. The doctors will be here as soon as they look at Ricky's x-rays."

We sit for just a few minutes, Dr. Derby's reading something in my folder; I recognize it. Suddenly four doctors come in a door at the right side of the room and sit at the table in front of us. They're all old.

Dr. Derby stands and introduces me and Mom to the doctors. No one's smiling except me. Dr. Derby talks about why he wants to do the surgery. He says he wants to stabilize my right foot to straighten it out and stop it from turning in. Dr. Derby told me it will turn in because it has no muscle. It has started to turn in and when I walk a lot it hurts a little on the outside of my foot. Dr. Derby finishes and now they're all looking at me.

"So, Ricky, what do you want to be when you grow up?" one of the doctors asks me.

This answer I know. "I'm going to be a teacher."

"A teacher!" the doctor bellows.

The doctors look at each other; they seem surprised with my answer. Dr. Derby doesn't seem surprised.

Another doctor asks, "Ricky, how do you think you're going to chase the kids around in the classroom when you walk on crutches?"

I'm shocked by his question. None of my teachers have to chase anybody. I wonder where he went to school.

I answer, "I won't have to."

The doctors look at each other again and mumble to each other. Dr. Derby's smiling. He knows I'll be a teacher someday. Finally, one of the doctors says thank you and tells us that they will have a decision in a few days. We all stand and Dr. Derby walks out into the hall with us. He says it went well and tells Mom he'll call her next week. On the way home I ask Mom to help me write the play. She says she will.

I've never had someone tell me I can't do something because I walk on crutches. I guess that doctor doesn't know me. I might be walking with a cane soon anyways. I love to teach. I've been helping Donna since she started school. Not that she needs help, I just like doing her homework with her.

CHAPTER 19

Loafers

~~

It was a long day today. It feels good to be in bed. I tried again to walk up the stairs onto the porch with my cane without using the railing, but my left leg still isn't strong enough. I can only do it if I hold onto the railing with my left hand and that puts me on the wrong side of the stairs. Mom says I'm going to have to practice more and we have to do more stretching and exercises of that left knee. Her words not mine—that left knee. Mom sounds like it's the enemy.

It's been two weeks today since I went to the library; my books are due. They're running out of books I like. Lucky it's almost a mile away or I'd have already read all the books I like in the library. None of the other kids I know like the library; I've always had to walk there alone. I don't understand people who don't like to read. My friends, even Larry, say it's a waste of time. Sure, they're off on their bikes; they don't have time to read. Time—I've got plenty of.

Let's see, I've finished all the Sherlock Holmes books, *Tarzan*, *The Hardy Boys*, and a bunch more. I've found a new series, but it's a secret. The series is about a girl named Pippi Longstocking. I hide those books between other books. They're girl's books; I tell the librarian they're for my sister. Pippi is so cool. She's strong enough to lift a horse and doesn't have to mind adults. She lives alone with her monkey, Mr. Nilsson, and her horse, Old Man. The library has three Pippi books and I've already read two. I hope the one I haven't read, *Pippi in the South Seas*, is there when I go.

"I talked with Ray; he says their tenant is moving late August."

I'm in bed listening to Mom and Dad.

Their tenant is moving. Is Dad talking about us moving across the street? Ray is Mary Anne's dad. Are we moving to the same house Mary Anne lives in?

"That's a good time," Mom says. "If Ricky's in a wheelchair its better we stay here on the first floor. I'll only have to carry him up and down the porch steps."

What're they talking about, a wheelchair—what's Mom mean by …? Oh yeah, if I have the operation.

"Can you wait that long to move?" Dad asks Mom.

"I guess we have no choice. We haven't heard any rats for a while anyways."

Wow, we're moving upstairs from Mary Anne. I can't believe it. God's definitely on my side.

Mom says, "Thank you for asking Ray. Is the rent cheaper?" I hope Dad asked.

"Yes, ten dollars less. We can use the extra money now that we're opening the garage."

Whew—he asked. What garage?

"I love you," Dad says.

"I love you too," Mom replies.

What about the garage; what was Dad talking about? Come on, keep talking. Oh, the commercial's over, I don't think I can stay awake till the next one. Guess I'll ask Dad tomorrow. What do I ask? I heard you say something about a garage last night? Then they'll know I listen. Guess I better wait until Dad says something.

Finally Mom and I are getting a chance to write the play. It's been almost a week.

"So what do you want the play to be about?" Mom asks me.

"It's going to be about a family that has a father and mother and three kids."

"Okay, what do you want them to do?"

"I want the father to be real forgetful. He keeps losing things like his shoes in the oven and his keys in the sink. He lost his briefcase for work and he keeps losing the other things while he's looking for the briefcase. His wife and kids find his shoes and keys and other things while they're helping him look, but they can't find the briefcase. At the end of the day, they finally give up and go to bed and in the morning when the father gets up he goes to take a shower and he comes back into the bedroom with his briefcase. It was in the bathtub."

"That sounds great, Ricky. Now we have to write the action and dialog."

Writing the play turns out to be a much bigger job than I thought. All this to get closer to Mary Anne, I hope it works. It takes us most of the day, but we're finally done.

"Okay, Ricky, now who do you want to be the actors?"

"Well, Ma." I have to be careful; I don't want to give it away.

"How about Rita, Cathy and Donna be the kids and I'll be the dad."

"That sounds good, but Rita's tall, so why can't she be the mom?"

Oh no, how do I get outta this?

"Well, Ma, that's a great idear, but she looks so young. We need someone who looks older. Who could that be?"

"Well the only one left is Mary Anne. Why don't you ask her to be the mom?"

"That sounds like a great idear! Thank you, Ma." Problem solved.

Now a new one, I'm not sure I can ask Mary Anne to be the mom. Got to talk to Donna.

"Thank you, Ma."

"You're welcome; that was fun."

"Yes it was," I answer, feeling very relieved that my motive hasn't been discovered and it was fun.

Donna must be in her room. The phone's ringing and Mom's got it. Yep here's Donna.

"Don, how would you like to be in a play?"

"Can I? What do I do?"

"Well, the first thing you do is talk to Rita, Cathy, and Mary Anne. You, Rita, and Cathy are going to be children and Mary Anne is going to be the mom. I need you to ask them to be in the play and tell them who they'll be."

"Okay, I'll ask them," Donna replies not realizing she's an accomplice.

"That's good; ask them tomorrow morning and tell me what they say."

"When are we going to have the play?"

"At the end of August. We're going to ask all the kids around here and their parents to come and see it. We need lots of time to practice and invite people."

I hear Mom hang up the phone. "Ricky, that was Dr. Derby, your operation will be on June 13th. You're going into the hospital the day before and if everything works out okay, you'll leave two weeks later. Dr. Derby says you'll be in the cast for two months. So you have a month."

If everything works out okay? So you have a month? What does that mean? Mom doesn't sound like she expects everything to not be okay. I wonder if she's worried.

I realize an opportunity here.

"Ma, I don't wear a shoe on the foot in the cast, do I?"

"No you don't, why?"

"Can I get loafers?"

Loafers are so cool, but I can't wear them with the brace. I have to have tie shoes. For two months I can have a loafer on my left foot.

"Your father and I will talk about it. We'll see."

Wow! Loafers—I'll look so cool. Loafers and practicing for the play, I can't miss.

It's a hot day and it's been uncomfortable in class. Larry and I don't get many chances to do anything after school, but this morning we agreed to meet and go across the street to the City Hospital. We went there last week on a hot day and it was so cool. We decided to go there again today to cool off. When we went there last week, we just wandered around the first floor and nobody bothered us. They probably thought I was a patient. The City Hospital is so much bigger than the other hospitals in the City. There's a big staircase made of stone about as wide as my house going up to six giant doors leading into a massive entrance with another wide stone staircase. At the top of the staircase there's a bunch of elevators and hallways to the left and right. There're offices in the hallways. Last week we just walked down the hallways. Today we're going to try the elevator.

Larry and I make our way across the street and walk through the parking lot in the front of the hospital and up the stairs. Larry opens one of the giant doors and we walk into the cool air. I wouldn't mind spending the night here in the hospital. We make it to the elevators. Again, no one asks us any questions. There's a counter with a receptionist. Last week we heard her giving visitors the room numbers and directions. Again today, she pays no attention to us. We walk up to one of the elevators and press the down button. I'm not sure why I pressed down. Probably because I know going up leads to the patient rooms. I've seen enough of those. The elevator door opens and Larry and I step on. We're alone.

"Okay, Larry where shall we go?"

"We'll if we're not going up, I guess our only choice is either the G or B button. Do you know what that means?"

"I'm not sure, so let's try the B button first."

The elevator door closes and we begin our slow descent. This elevator seems so much slower and definitely quieter than the one at Dr. Derby's. With little warning, the elevator slows to a stop and the door abruptly opens. Larry and I are immediately overcome with heat and steam and noise. The noise is deafening and the heat and steam immediately fill the elevator and our lungs. We look at each other in panic.

I yell, "It's Hell!" I reach in a panic for another button, any button. I finally press one and after what seems forever, the door closes and the elevator starts its slow ascent. We're both standing in the elevator in a state of shock, my heart beating so hard I can feel it in my ears. We look at each other wondering what we've just experienced when I realize.

"Larry, that was the laundry; the B is for basement." We laugh and poke each other as the elevator arrives at our starting point, the first floor, back to safety. My heart is still beating hard and fast. We've got to find a place to sit for a while.

Well that mystery's solved. Dad told Donna and me this morning that he's opening a garage with Earl on the other side of the City near Bob. Earl is the man in the house behind Wieland's. His wife's name is Eleanor. I went to school in Town with their daughter, Marianne. I'd like to see her again. She's so pretty.

Dad says he's going to work nights at the garage and Earl will work days. Dad's going to continue working at Auto Gear until they get enough business for Dad to work only at the garage. I guess we won't get to see him much. We're going to the garage tomorrow night to see it. I wonder if I can pump gas someday. Mom and Dad said I can have the loafers. Everything's working out great except the operation. Wish I could skip that part and still get the loafers. Don't think I'll think about it now—there is a problem that could change everything.

We're on our way to the garage. Dad says we've only got a little ways to go.

"Dad, can I pump gas?"

"Not yet, Son, you're not old enough; maybe someday."

Okay, I've planted the idear.

"How old do you have to be to pump gas?"

"Sixteen and not before," Mom says in her *and don't ask again* voice.

"Here it is," Dad says as we pull into a gas station.

It's dark. There're no lights on except for a small light in the office area. Dad parks right in front of the office. Another car is pulling in behind us. It's Earl and Eleanor and Marianne's with them. Wow, she's prettier than ever and she's … well I guess you could say grown up more—not taller—more grown up. She's coming my way.

"Hi, Ricky," she says with a smile.

"Hi, Marianne," I respond, trying to sound cool.

I didn't even know she knew my name. Dad's unlocking the door and everyone's talking. Dad's carrying Donna, her favorite place and I think the safest here. It smells a lot like Auto Gear in here. There're two big garage doors and a lift to pick up cars. I can't wait to spend time here.

"Dad, when do you start working here?"

"Earl opens in two weeks on a Monday. I start that night."

"Can I come and help on the weekend?"

"I don't think so, Ricky; not yet." Dad's *not yet* sounds more like never.

I hope that doesn't happen, I really want to work here. Marianne's touching everything and looking at her fingers. She's making faces and smiling at me. I smile back, but I don't know what to say to her. Boy she's pretty. She looks a lot more than two years older than me.

Dad and Earl have been in the station for a month now. They're talking about hiring a boy to pump gas at night, so Dad has time to fix cars. They don't have enough business yet, but that's what they're going to do. I wish I was 16. Tomorrow I go into the hospital for my operation. Mom says she, Aunt Ruth, and Uncle Al will visit me during the day and she and Aunt Ruth will visit at night. Donna's going to stay at the Segal's. They've got this all planned out, but what about if I die during the operation? Is that planned for? Is that all planned out? That would spoil everything. We've already bought my loafers. I hope I get a chance to wear them, they're so cool.

CHAPTER 20

Ether

Dad took the day off today from Auto Gear and the gas station. I'm walking between Mom and Dad up the walk to the Our Lady Hospital front doors. I've never been so scared, but I can't tell anyone. They'll think I'm a baby. My arms feel like loose rubber bands as I put my weight on my hands. I guess this is how people feel when they say their knees went weak. I feel it in my arms. My arms don't want to propel my legs forward. Why am I working so hard to get closer to those doors? This is it, Dad's opening the door. I have to step into the hospital. Do I have a choice? No! Marty didn't know any better.

Check in is over and all the papers are signed. I know the routine. Different hospital but so far the same routine. We're at the second floor, the elevator stops, and the doors open. That same smell, Wally said it's the cleaner they use to keep the hospital safe for all the sick people. We step off the elevator.

"Mr. and Mrs. Willett?"

"Yes," Mom says. "I'm Sister Helen. Please follow me and I'll show you to the ward."

It's a nun. That's different, it's usually a nurse. We walk into a large room like the children's ward at the Weston with all the cribs. Dad stops.

"There must be a mistake."

"A mistake?" Sister Helen questions.

"Yes," Dad says. "He's not staying in the children's ward. He doesn't need a crib anymore."

"Yes," Sister Helen says, "but your son isn't big enough to be in a room with beds."

"What?" Mom says with surprise. "He's eleven years old. He doesn't belong in a crib."

"I'm sorry you feel that way, Mrs. Willett, that's our policy."

This is going nowhere. Sister Helen isn't at all concerned. She sounds like this makes sense. This is the end. I'm so afraid and now they want to put me in a crib.

"Ma, I'm not going to sleep in a crib!"

"I'm sorry, young man, but there are no options. If you're going to stay in this hospital, it's going to be in this ward."

She's not going to give in. Mom and Dad are just looking at each other. I know what's coming. Dad squats to my level.

"Ricky, I'm sorry, Son. It's only for two weeks and then you're home."

What am I going to say? Nothing, I can see I don't have a choice.

"Here's Ricky's crib and this is his gown. He can wear his own pajamas after he has surgery."

Dad picks me up and places me on the crib mattress. I'm glad no one from school can see me here, especially Mary Anne.

It's morning and I'm not getting breakfast. I love hospital food and I don't think I'll be eating any for a while. Mom says I'll be eating soon after the surgery. I wish I was that sure that I would be eating again. Mom and Dad should be here soon. They said they'd come before I go to surgery. Here's a man with a stretcher. I hope he's not looking for me; I'm not ready. He's looking over at me and heading in my direction.

"Good morning, Ricky. Are you ready for your surgery?"

"I can't go yet; my Mom and Dad are coming."

"Well, it'll take a few minutes to get you on this stretcher, but the doctor is waiting for you upstairs."

The nurse comes in the ward and walks over to me and the man. "That's your boy. He's already to go."

I grab my right leg with my right hand and grab the inside crib rail with my left. I draw my arms and my left leg in so that I'm a tight ball against the rail. I'm not going anywhere yet.

The man says, "Ricky, the doctor is waiting, he has a schedule to keep. You'll see your Mom and Dad after surgery."

No way, he's going to have to break my arms to get me out of here. "Ma!" They're here.

"We're sorry. We had a little trouble downstairs. It's not visiting time and they said we couldn't come up."

I let go of the rail and let the man lift me onto the stretcher.

"We'll be here when you come back," Mom says as the man pushes me out of the ward toward the elevator.

Dad has an arm around Mom. They don't look very happy today. I'm being pushed down the hall covered and strapped down. I guess they want to make sure I don't try to escape. It's a short ride up to the floor where they do the operations.

The man pushes me into a room like I've never seen before. It has a table in the middle of the room and shiny metal equipment all around. There's a big round lamp above the table. The lamp's not on. They're no windows, just doors. They're four nuns waiting.

"Good morning, Ricky," one of the nuns says cheerfully.

"Good morning," I reply, faking cheerful.

The man undoes the straps, takes the blanket off of me, and lifts me onto the table. Everything feels cold. I'm shivering from the cold and my heart is beating so hard. I don't ever remember being this afraid.

Another man comes in the room and smiles at me. "Good morning, Ricky. I'm Dr. Moriarty. I'm going to take care of you during your surgery, but first I have to put you to sleep."

The doctor is standing at the head of the table with his stomach against the top of my head. What's that in his hand? It looks like the strainer Mom uses to strain the seeds out of the lemon juice when she makes lemonade. There're two nuns on each side of me. Why are they here?

"Now I'm just going to put this over your nose and mouth. The doctor puts the palm of his hand with the strainer under my chin and holds my head tight against him. I can't move my head. What's that smell? The strainer, it smells so bad. It's gagging me. I can't move. The nuns are holding me down. The doctor is dripping something from a bottle onto the strainer. I can't breathe. He's killing me.

"Ricky, now take a deep breath."

He's killing me. I close my eyes struggling to get away. The four nuns tighten their grip. I see a light, it's getting bigger. It's gone, everything's black. I see writing in white against the black: Richard You Are Going To Sleep.

CHAPTER 21

The Saw

~⦿

"Ricky, Ricky! Wake up." That smell, it's so bad. "Ricky, wake up."

"Ma, Dad."

Oh, my foot it hurts and that terrible smell.

"What's that smell; what is it?"

Dad leans over me and sniffs. "That's ether. They used ether to put you to sleep. It's okay, Son. Haven't you smelled that before? I've used it a few times in the winter to start the car.

"It was terrible." I respond as I reach down to try to move my right leg, but it's hard and too heavy.

"No, Honey, don't move that leg," Mom says gently. "They put a cast on your leg."

"It hurts, Ma."

"I know," Mom says. "It'll feel better soon."

Mom and Dad look happy again. I hurt, but I made it. I wish I could touch my foot.

"Ma."

"Yes, Honey."

"When can I wear my loafer?"

"As soon as they get you up and in a wheelchair."

~⦿

It's been a couple of weeks now and I'm still in this crib. Not much longer, maybe a few days more. Today the cast comes off for a little while. Dr. Derby's taking the stitches out. I wonder what that feels like. My foot hasn't hurt for over a week now, but nobody tells you the cast's going to itch and I can barely reach where it itches the most. It feels so good to slide the knitting needle Aunt Ruth gave me down into the cast and scratch.

What a wonderful feeling except when I can't reach the itch. Mom doesn't like me to scratch because she thinks I'll cut myself. There're times I'd be happy to stick the sharp end of a pencil into my leg, anything to relieve the itch. The right side of my foot near where Dr. Derby did the surgery itches the most, but I can't scratch there. Dr. Derby says it won't itch as much after he takes out the stitches.

Here comes the guy with my ride to get my cast off. The cast room is on the first floor near the emergency room. It's a small room with a table in the center and lots of cabinets with glass doors and a sink. There's cast dust all over. There's a man in the room wearing a white coat like the doctors wear.

"Hi, Ricky, I'm Jack. So we're going to cut your cast off today are we?"

Cut off! What's this cut off?

"This is the saw we use and what I want to show you is how the saw doesn't cut skin only hard material like the cast."

He turns the saw on and puts the blade on his palm and nothing happens to his skin. The saw is so loud. He might be sure it's not going to cut me, but I'm not convinced. I can't help but tense up. Jack tries to move my left leg out of the way.

"Ricky, you can relax, I promise it won't hurt."

Easy for him to say. Jack presses the blade against the bottom inside of the cast right next to my big toe. I can just see my toe falling to the floor and blood shooting all over. The growl of the saw is deafening as Jack presses down on the thick areas around my ankle. The saw whines and growls as it throws dust all over the room and me. Finally, the saw gets past my ankle to where the cast is thinner. It's moving fast toward my knee.

Jack's almost done with the first side. In short order Jack finishes cutting the other side and lifts the top part of the cast off of my leg. What's left of what looks like a cotton wrapping on my leg under the cast is wet with sweat. Ah … the cool air settling on my leg feels so good. That wasn't so bad. Here's Dr. Derby.

"Hi, Ricky."

"Hi, Dr. Derby."

"How was that?"

"Not bad," I answer, but I really want to know how it's going to feel to get the stitches out.

No use asking. I've learned that the answer's never helpful. May as well just wait and find out. Dr. Derby gently lifts my leg out of the bottom half of the cast, picks up a pair of surgical scissors, and starts to cut off the cotton wrapping on my leg and the bandage wrapped around my ankle. It's then that I see the patch of dried blood that soaked through the bandage on the outside of my ankle.

I finally get to see my foot and it looks terrible. It's shades of yellow, orange and violet.

"Why's my foot look like that?"

"That's the antiseptic and dried blood," Dr. Derby says.

A nun has joined us and she begins to gently wash my foot with soap and warm water. It feels so good after its confinement. I suddenly think of Mary washing Jesus' feet. It makes me chuckle. The nun smiles.

"Is your foot ticklish?"

"Yes," I tell her; I'm not sure she'd appreciate the image I have.

I notice that there's a tender spot on the outside of my foot just below my ankle. I can't see it yet, but I imagine it's the scar.

"Can I see the scar?"

"Sure," says the nun as she gently turns my leg.

It's about four inches long and its tender. Around the scar it feels numb in some spots but very sensitive in others. Finally, the nun, who I now know is Sister Joan, finishes washing my foot and leg. Now it's time to take out the stitches, here goes.

Dr. Derby's holding what looks like little wire cutters and tweezers.

"I'm going to cut the stitch and pull it through; you won't feel much," Dr. Derby says without looking at me.

I can't think of a single thing to say except, can we do this another time. I doubt Dr. Derby would appreciate my humor. He's grabbing the first stitch with the tweezers and lifting. Oh, I hate this. I can't move that leg or foot. I hate that it's so defenseless. I don't like anybody to touch my right foot when they're holding cutting tools, even toenail clippers. Dr. Derby cuts the stitch and pulls it through. He's right, it doesn't hurt. It feels funny. Finally, Dr. Derby finishes. He lifts my foot to inspect the scar and then gently sets it down onto the table.

"Time to put a new cast on," Dr. Derby says as he puts on an apron that covers him from his neck to almost his knees. The apron is longer on Jack.

Is he going to help Jack? No, he's putting a cast on me! I guess he wants to be sure the foot's okay. That wasn't so bad. I can feel my entire body relax. The knots in my stomach slowly untie. I'm that much closer to wearing that loafer.

CHAPTER 22

The Walk

The summer's over, I got to wear the loafer, the cast is off, the play's been performed, and nothing's changed. Mary Anne made a great mom in the play. It seemed like the girls were really mother and daughters, but Mary Anne never warmed up to me. The loafer had no effect. All the neighbors liked the play and the girls liked being in the play, but it didn't solve my problem. Mary Anne and I barely talked during the rehearsals. She was friendly, but never wanted to talk to me about anything but the play. What do you say to a girl you have such a crush on, but she barely acknowledges your existence?

Mary Anne likes the boy down the street. He doesn't pay any attention to her; she must feel like I do. Maybe she doesn't know I like her? Should I tell her? No way—that will definitely get a reaction from her and I'm afraid it won't be a good one. She'll either laugh or be angry. What does a boy do when this happens, first Cindy and now Mary Anne? Next week we move across the street, which should help. Mary Anne and I will be living in the same house. Her bedroom is going to be right below mine.

We're going to Normie's. He still lives in Town, but they've moved to a part of the town called the North End. Pepe lives in the North End too. Today's the last day for making crafts at the grammar school near Normie. That's where Dad went to grammar school. I brought my cane to try walking to the school. We're at Normie's and he's outside waiting. I can't wait to try walking that far with the cane. Its five blocks to the school and it's uphill the whole way. Normie and Donna are ready and we're on our way. Walking uphill's not too hard. It's actually easier than walking downhill. My leg is stronger when my knee is bent a little.

Bending my knee to walk up a stair step is too much, but walking up this hill is much easier than walking downhill. It's the same when I'm walking on a sidewalk that's tilted; it's easier for me to walk with the cane when my left leg is on the uphill side. We're at the top of the hill. All we have to do is cross the street and walk up the drive to the picnic tables on the side of the school. There're a lot of kids already sitting at the tables. Walking across the street and up the drive isn't so easy. My leg is very tired and my left butt hurts from trying to keep that left leg from collapsing; I think I'll sit down and help Normie and Donna do a craft.

We work for an hour and Normie and Donna have made key rings for Dad and Uncle Norm. It's time to start downhill. Getting down the drive and across the street wasn't too bad, but walking downhill is much harder. We've gone only two blocks and I've got to stop. My leg is shaking so hard when I put my weight on it.

"Hold it, Normie and Donna. I've got to stop for a minute; I don't want to overwork this leg," I say with a smile, I don't want to scare them.

Maybe if I hold my hand against my thigh it will support me a little. Normie and Donna are too young to run home by themselves. I've got to make it.

"Okay, let's go."

Half a block and it's shaking again, my butt hurts so much. Just a little farther and we'll be able to see the house around the corner. Oh, it almost gave out. I need to talk with them, so they don't worry that I'm not going to make it.

"Okay, let's stop just a few more minutes. Did you have fun making the key rings?"

"Yes," Normie and Donna say together. They look worried.

"Gig, are you going to get home?" Donna asks. She uses her childhood nickname for me. I can hear the fear in her voice and see it on her face. She'll feel better when she can see Normie's house.

"Yes, Honey. Don't worry, I'm okay."

This close—we're almost there, and I'm not sure I'm going to make it.

"Okay, let's go."

Just a little farther, we're past half way. Just one more block and one more street to cross and we can see Normie's house. When we get to Normie's block, I'll tell them to run ahead and show Dad and Uncle Norm the key rings. I'll hang onto the fences to get the rest of the way.

I see Normie's house. "There's the house," I tell them.

I can't believe I made it this far. All we have to do is walk a half a block, cross the street and I can let them go.

We've made it to the street. "Let's stop here before we cross the street. When we get across, you can run and give Dad and Uncle Norm their key rings. I'll catch up to you."

I hope I don't fall in the middle of the street. My leg and butt feel numb and hurt at the same time. It's never felt this bad at therapy.

"Okay, let's cross the street." The street goes up until we reach the middle. This part is a little easier. I've made it to the middle of the street, it's downhill again. I don't want to collapse here in the road. I don't think I'll be able to get up. Oh, that step was hard. Now my arm that's pushing against my thigh is shaking as much as my leg, just a little farther. Three more steps, two more steps, one more step. We're at the curb. I hope I can get up onto the sidewalk.

"Okay, you can run ahead now."

There they go, screeching with excitement. They can't wait to deliver those key rings. Time to try to get off the street and onto the sidewalk. Nope, both of my arms and my leg are shaking. Rest a little more. If I sit down on the curb, I'm not sure I'll be able to get back up. It's too close to the corner anyways, cars stop here at the stop sign. I better try again before they start to worry about me and come looking for me. I don't want anybody to know. One more try. Okay, push. I made it. It's a little uphill to the fence. I got it. Now I can get to the driveway, it's uphill to the car and my crutches. I'm not sure the cane will ever replace my crutches. I hope it will.

Today's a grocery shopping day. I hate these days. When the weather's warm enough, Donna and I sit in the car. We sat in the car most of last spring, summer, and fall almost every Friday evening and now again this year. Mom and Dad like to shop together. I don't blame them for wanting to be alone; Dad works all the time. We've not had time to play catch since we moved to the City. I don't like sitting here in the car waiting for Mom and Dad to come out of the store, it scares me. I don't understand why. It doesn't make sense. Donna and I are playing Go Fish.

"Do you have a five?"

"No, Don, go fish."

She loves this game and she likes sitting in the car, but I can't control this fear. I shake, sweat, and my stomach is tied in knots. It's hard to play cards with Donna; I can barely concentrate. Every time we do this, I can't help the feeling that Mom and Dad aren't coming back. It doesn't make sense. I'm never afraid when I leave the house or I'm at someone else's house and Mom and Dad leave, only when Mom and Dad leave us in the car. I don't want Donna to know how I feel, it'll scare her.

"Do you have any sixes?"

Donna gives me one. It's tough smiling through this. I don't want to scare Donna and Mom and Dad would think I'm a baby if they knew how I feel. I'm twelve now, I shouldn't be afraid. It just doesn't seem to be getting any better.

"Do you have any sevens?"

"You got me Donna. I've got two." Oh, finally, here come Mom and Dad.

～੭

Sunday school today and then Fred and I go to the movies. Today we're going to see "The Blob." It's a scary movie and I'm not sure I can watch it. I hid my eyes during the preview last week. Going to the movies and playing war on the way home is the best thing Fred and I get to do. No, being with Fred doing anything is best. I get stomach aches a lot now and the only time I don't feel them is when I'm with Fred. I should probably tell Mom and Dad about these stomach aches. I'll wait a little longer, maybe they'll stop.

Aunt Net got smart. She put Fred and me across from each other on either side of her. This is our last year in Sunday school. I guess she's decided we're going to learn something or else. Just a few more minutes and we're outta here, to lunch and then the movie.

"Okay, children, that's enough for today."

We're out! Fred and I can't get out fast enough, Dad's waiting for us. When we get to Fred's, it's peanut butter and jelly sandwiches, our favorite. Fred and I wolf our sandwiches down and bolt outta the house. It's three blocks to the theater and it would be faster with the wagon, but we don't dare leave it outside the theater. Plus it would be in the way when we play war; I'd be an easy target.

Okay, we've got our candy. Now that we come to the movies, we get real candy every week and now I know what Peanut Butter Cups are like. Today it's Rolos for me and we've got our favorite seats, in the middle of the theater. The first thing is the previews. Lots of kids here; this is going to be a great movie, if I can watch it.

"Hey, Fred, let's go through the fence behind the Post Office when we chase the Germans today."

"Yeah, that way's the best. We'll chase them into the trees. I hope there're no snipers today," Fred says as if our imaginary German soldiers are real.

Our moms say our imaginations are too active. I guess they think we make up too many things. Making up is so much easier. Last week we tried to make a real go-kart and that didn't work out. We found some boards and crates and Fred had four wheels in the cellar. We had to beg for nails and a hammer. I knew that pounding the wheels onto the end of a board with nails wasn't going to be strong enough. We actually got the go-kart together and it rolled just fine, but it only lasted until Fred sat in it. The nails bent on all four wheels. It was fun, but nothing breaks when we use our imagination. We can play war and travel to outer space in our ship. Fred's bedroom is a great spaceship. We travel to strange places throughout the universe. The movie's starting.

"Here we go, Fred."

Boy this is going to be great. I think I'll keep my hand under my chin and rest my head on it.

"Are you going to put your hand over your eyes through this whole movie?" Fred says.

"No, I'm just resting my head!"

"You're slouching in your seat too."

"I know, it's easier to rest my head."

I hope Fred's not going to be after me through this whole movie. I know the Blob isn't real, but it seemed so real in the preview or at least the split second look I got before I covered my eyes. I'll try to watch.

Hey this looks like a love story not a horror movie, a boy and girl kissing in a car. There's a meteor, it crashes. Okay, now we're getting somewhere. Hey, old man get back in the house. Here it is night time and he's out looking for the meteor. We know something's going to happen, why can't he? I've got an itch on my forehead. Think I'll scratch it slowly.

"What are you doing, Rick?"

"I've got an itch on my forehead, I'm scratching it."

"No you're not, you're hiding your eyes."

"What's he doing, Fred?"

"He's poking the meteor with a stick. Hey, it's cracking open, the inside looks like one of your Rolos."

The movie's over and I never did see it. I did see one scene where there was a sign in the doctor's office that said polio. That was just before the Blob ate the doctor. I missed that part. Fred said the movie wasn't so scary. Sure, for him. Now it's time to play war. I hope Dad's at Fred's when we get home. He worked at the station again today. Last night I heard him tell Mom that he's not sure how long they can last. The way he said it scared me. I'm not sure what he was talking about.

I didn't hear what he said in the beginning and they stopped talking after he said it. What can't last?

Dad's job at Auto Gear didn't last. He has a new job just like the one he had at Auto Gear and it's near where we used to live in Town. We moved to the City, so he was closer to work and now he doesn't work there anymore. So what can't last now?

CHAPTER 23

Station Closing

~⌐

"**R**icky, Donna, come here for a moment; Mom and I have something to tell you."

A surprise, I wonder. No, Dad didn't sound happy, what have we done?

"What's the matter, Dad?"

"I'll tell you as soon as Donna gets here."

Come on, Donna, I'm getting nervous; I need to hear this. Here she comes. Look at that look on her face. She looks so guilty. Donna slowly sits down beside me; she's guilty of something.

"Kids, I've got good news and bad news. First the good news, Dad's going to be home nights and weekends from now on."

Oh no … and the bad? "The bad news is that we're closing the garage. Well maybe that isn't bad news."

I knew it! I never got to go there and work. We hung out a few times waiting for Dad to finish some work, but that's not the same. Okay, I'm happy Dad's going to be home, but I knew it. Mom and Dad are holding hands. I think Mom's happy; I don't think Dad is. Mom's actually holding Dad's hand in her hands.

"I've got to go and get my tools and lock up the garage, and when I get back we'll all go out for ice cream."

"Can I go with you, Dad?"

"No, Ricky, it's pretty dirty in the garage. I'll be back soon."

I knew it, stay here with Mom and Donna. Dad's gone; I wonder how he feels.

"Ma, is Dad unhappy about the garage?"

"Yes he is, Ricky; this isn't the first time."

"It isn't?"

"No, your father and a friend opened a station in the City when you were little, right after we got the car, but he got sick and couldn't continue.

"When he was in the hospital?"

"Yes. Your father's always wanted to have a business, but it hasn't worked out."

"Are you sad for Dad?"

"Yes, I'm sad for your Dad."

I don't know what to feel. I wanted to be at the station and then I would be with Dad. Maybe he'll open another gas station someday.

"Ricky."

"Yeah, Ma."

"Tomorrow, Dad and I have an appointment in the afternoon, then you're going to stay at Uncle Carl's with Peanut."

"Okay," I answer, happy to be somewhere else for a while. Best part, I've never stayed at Peanut's before. Oh yeah, it sounds like Donna and I will be in the car alone again.

We're leaving for Mom and Dad's appointment. Mom asked us to get a book and she's got some games. It looks like Donna and I are waiting in the car again. Dad's parking the car.

"Okay, kids, Mom and I are going in that business right there and we'll be out soon. Sit tight and play some games or read," Dad says getting out of the car.

I see the business sign, Household Finance. I wonder what kind of business that is. I can see the front door of the business. Mom and

Dad can't leave without me seeing them. I wonder if they have a back door. Why do I always have these thoughts? I hate this feeling. My stomach hurts. I can't believe Donna doesn't notice. I'm sure my voice shakes when I talk to her.

"Ricky, can we play a game?"

"Don, why don't you read for a little while, look at the pictures."

I hope Mom and Dad are coming out soon. This is the same road we live on. We're not far from Auto Gear, the Weston Hospital, and Dr. Derby's. They're coming back soon, I know they are. Why do I feel this way?

"Gig, can we play a game now?" She's not going to stop. I don't want to take my eyes off the front door of the business.

"Okay, let's play Go Fish." I can watch the door over the cards. I feel guilty that I think Mom and Dad would leave us here. That's a stupid thought; I know they never would.

Here they come … oh that feels better! Seeing them is such a relief. I thought they'd never come out the door.

"Hi, Mom. Hi, Dad." I'm so happy to see them.

I wish I could get over this. I don't know anyone my age that feels this way. Dad and Mom turn and look at me and Donna.

Mom says, "Kids, don't ever tell anyone we came here. Do you understand?"

"Yes, Ma," we say in unison.

"Why not, Ma?" I ask.

Mom and Dad look at each other and Dad says, "Well Mom and Dad had to borrow some money to pay debts from the garage and we don't want anyone to know."

I hear it, but I don't understand why no one else can know. What I do know is that I'll keep the secret; Mom and Dad look so unhappy.

"Are we going to Peanut's now?" I ask, ready to be somewhere else.

"We are, Ricky," Dad says. I feel so much better. We're all together again even if it's only till we get to Peanut's.

Peanut lives on the first floor of a two family house like the house we live in. The house seems older than ours. It needs paint. The other houses nearby look older too. Peanut's waiting on the front porch.

"Hi, Peanut."

"Hi, Rick, come on in; Dad's making supper."

We join Uncle Carl in the kitchen. He's older than Dad and he looks older because he's losing his hair. Uncle Carl also acts older. When he talks to Dad, he acts and sounds like he's talking to his younger brother. Dad doesn't seem to mind. In fact, I think he enjoys it. Everyone in Dad's family treats Uncle Carl like he's special. He does seem very wise to me and carefree. Uncle Carl may be a wise man, but he's not much of a decorator. There isn't a piece of furniture that matches. There're curtains in the windows, but they're very plain. The house is clean, but it's obvious that a woman doesn't live here; Peanut's mom died when he was born.

Peanut's a lot of fun; he doesn't have many rules like I do. He gets to stay up late and miss school sometimes when he's not sick. Uncle Carl works, so Peanut takes care of himself a lot. I like Peanut's life, it's kind of like Pipi's, but I like having a mom. Mom and Dad are talking with Uncle Carl; they're not staying for dinner. Dad's standing in the kitchen holding Donna. Does that girl ever walk?

"You boys be good for your father and uncle," Mom says as she opens the door. "Make sure you're in bed early." I knew she'd say that.

"See you later, Son," Dad says. I can tell by his tone that he's thinking what I'm thinking; Mom can't let it be.

Uncle Carl's the man of the family and he looks funny in an apron. He always wears one when he cooks. I don't think anyone would tell him it looks funny, I know I'm not. He wouldn't get mad, but it just wouldn't be right. He's a gentle man like Uncle Al. The only difference is that Uncle Carl sometimes seems lonely.

We finish dinner. Uncle Carl made spaghetti and meatballs. It was really good. Peanut always eats like it's his last meal and he's as skinny as a pole. It's probably because he can't sit still. I know he makes Mom nervous because he has to touch everything and he's up and down from chair to chair and room to room; Uncle Carl's more relaxed. He usually has a beer in his hand and talks about anything that comes to his mind. Dad works too much to sit and talk and he doesn't drink beer unless we're at a party. I've never seen Uncle Carl drink so much that I felt uncomfortable. I can't say the same for all my Uncles. Uncle Carl just seems to get happier and more fun. Tonight we're gonna play card games and have cake and soda. I know we're gonna stay up late, very late.

It actually seems lonely here even though we're having a good time. It's not like it was at Aunt Ruth and Uncle Al's when they lived in the fourth floor apartment. When I looked out the window at night the City seemed lonely, but here it feels lonely inside. Is it because there's not a wife and mom here? I remember it was lonely when Mom worked at night.

CHAPTER 24

The Fall

~○

"Uncle Carl, Uncle Carl! My stomach."
I just woke up to the smell of bacon and eggs and my stomach hurts so much. I can't straighten out.

"Please call my Ma." Oh! I hurt so much.

"Do you feel sick?" Uncle Carl asks.

"No, I just hurt." My stomach hurts much more than it did when I ate the ant poison.

Uncle Carl's calling Mom. I know he hates to have to do it; Mom's going to think its Uncle Carl's fault. I know it's not. I don't feel sick to my stomach; I just hurt.

Mom and Dad finally arrive. I still can't straighten up. Mom sits on the bed beside me.

"Has it gotten any better since Uncle Carl called?"

"No." I don't feel like talking; it hurts.

"What did you have to eat last night?"

Thank God, Uncle Carl answers for me, "We had spaghetti and meatballs, cake, and soda. Oh yes, we also had popcorn."

"Do you feel like you could get sick," Mom asks.

"No, Ma, I just hurt real bad."

"Okay, we're going to go to the hospital."

Dad carries me into the emergency room. I can't uncurl. It still hurts as much as it did when I woke. Finally, a doctor comes in to look at me.

"Can you straighten out, Ricky?"

"No."

"Can you try a little?" he asks.

I straighten out a little and he starts to press around my stomach. It hurts and my body wants to curl up. The doctor asks Mom a bunch of questions and says they're going to take me for an x-ray. It takes what seems forever, but I'm finally back with Mom and Dad. The doctor comes in and tells Mom and Dad that they didn't see anything in the x-ray and they're going to keep me and run some more tests. He says he called a specialist, Mom says it's a stomach specialist. I wonder if this has anything to do with the pains I get in my stomach, the ones that go away when I'm with Fred.

I like the taste of the green medicine the doctor gave us. I have to take it every morning. Mom says I'm going to have to take the medicine for a while. Mom's *a while* can be one week or years. That's what she says about therapy and I've been going 10 years now. Mom says a while when I ask her how long we're going to be at the store. I hope we're never at the store for 10 years. Mom says the valve at the top of my stomach isn't working right and that's why I had that pain. The green medicine will make it better. I'm glad it tastes good, but I'd take it if it didn't; anything would be better than that pain. I had that dream again last night, the one about the building. That can go away anytime. I wish they had medicine for it.

I'm at Pepe's this weekend because Mom and Dad are moving to the apartment above the Segal's. It's almost as big as the one we were in, and Mr. Segal says it's rat free. I can't wait to live there, so I can check out the small barn behind the house; it has stalls in it. There's also a metal post in the front of the house with a small statue of a horse and rider on top of the post. Mr. Segal said the barn is where people kept their horses and the post is where people in horse drawn carriages hitched their horses. These must be old houses: the ice box in the house we're moving from—a barn and hitching post at the house we're moving to.

Mom and Dad have just arrived at Pepe's and Mom sees I'm holding a picture Pepe gave me. It's a picture of Jesus painted on a regular size sheet of paper. Jesus has long hair and a beard. It's just a picture of His face staring out from the paper. Mom takes the picture from me and smiles but doesn't give it back. Mom and Dad stay long enough to have coffee. We get in the car and start to drive away. Mom turns sideways in the front seat and looks back at me.

"Ricky, in our church we don't keep pictures or statues of God or Jesus."

"I know, Ma, but Pepe gave it to me."

"I didn't say you can't keep it; you can hang it on the wall above the head of your bed. I just want you to understand that, when you pray, you're praying to God and Jesus, not a picture. The picture could become an idol like that good luck piece you had."

Fred plays basketball for the team at church and I go and watch. I had a little plastic man that I had in my pocket when the team won their first game and I started thinking that the toy was a good luck piece. Mom saw me holding it at a game and asked me why I was holding the man so tight in my hand. I told her it was a good luck piece. It was then that Mom explained that I was treating the toy like an idol.

"I understand, Ma."

Mom reaches over the seat and gives the picture back to me.

When we get home, I find a tack and hang the picture above my bed. I love the picture. I don't know if it's because Pepe gave it to me or I like the feeling that He's close.

Sixth grade's been a lot different than any of the others. It's the first time I have a friend that's a girl. If I like a girl, I want to be her boyfriend but not Grace. I just like being with her and talking with her. She's funny. She has a lot of hair and it's so curly. I'd say it's like a clown because it's kind of red and so curly, but Grace isn't a clown. She's very serious, yet she does like to laugh at my comments. In sixth grade we sit at tables. There're three tables in the room and eight of us sit around each table. Grace sits right next to me. I've never sat this close to someone in class. We get to help each other a lot. She's better at spelling and writing and I'm better at math and history. Grace says she's Russian Orthodox. It took me a while to figure out it's a religion. I never heard of it. I think it means she's Russian. We're not friends with the Russians in this country, but Grace is nice. She seems kind of mysterious being Russian.

Girls have always been a problem. Things aren't so simple and they've got a lot more complicated. It all started last week when I was waiting for Mom and Dad on the front steps. It was going to be *a while*, maybe years. Rita was playing in her dad's car. She was getting ready to take her dolls for a ride and wanted me to be the husband and drive us to the country. She was putting the dolls on the passenger side and she was going to sit in the middle. Rita wanted me to get in the driver's side next to her. Of course, we really weren't going anywhere. I tried to think of an excuse to get out of it, but I was trapped. It didn't seem right to just say no, so I got in the car with her.

Rita's a year younger than me, but she's tall for her age, so you wouldn't notice she's younger. Sitting next to me she looked so pretty. Long dark hair tied in a ponytail, big dark brown eyes, and her skin tanned by the summer sun even though summer's been over for a month. I tried to ignore how pretty she was and how close we were; our arms touched. That's when it happened—I got this strange feeling—it's hard to explain. I felt warm and something ... I don't know what. I never felt this way before. I was so scared I had to get outta the car as fast as I could. I said my Mom was coming and I struggled to get my crutches out between the seat and the door. I almost fell out of the car.

⁓

"Okay, Rick, let's get him out," Fred says with confidence.

It's Saturday afternoon and Fred, Uncle Jerry and I are playing baseball. This is the first pitch of the game and we want to get Uncle Jerry out quick. It's not likely, but we're gonna try. We're playing the baseball game that Uncle Jerry made up. We use a Whiffle ball and bat and we don't run the bases or break windows; I only have to pitch and hit. I love to hit but pitching not so much because Uncle Jerry never strikes out. He was a wrestling and football star in high school and now he plays football in college; he's a running back. Uncle Jerry thought up how to play in the backyard where a single, double, triple, and home run is decided by the distance the ball travels or where it goes in the field. The ball striking or going over things in the field can be a home run or an out.

There's a fence two backyards away in left field that's an automatic home run and the fence in the backyard in right field is an out. If the ball hits the garage in the backyard, it's an out. If the ball goes over the garage, it's a home run. Fred and I can barely ever get the ball over the garage. Fred and I get the ball over the right field fence often and we hit the garage a lot, but only Uncle Jerry can get it over the fence two backyards away in left field. Fred's getting close. On our team, I pitch and Fred covers the field. Uncle Jerry does it all on his team.

"Okay, Fred, here comes a strike," I yell and we both laugh, so hard I can't pitch.

"All right, Ricky, let's see what you've got," Uncle Jerry says a little impatiently.

I finally compose myself and throw the ball. Uncle Jerry hits a fly ball and Fred gets underneath it. He got it, one out, two more to go.

Today's Sunday and it's a big day for me and Fred. It's children's Sunday and Fred and I are graduating from Sunday school. I'm looking forward to graduating and getting our Bibles with our names written in gold on the cover but not to having to recite the Bible verse I had to memorize. I've been practicing it for weeks and I'm still having trouble remembering all of it. I don't want to make a fool of myself in front of everybody in church. Fred's got his memorized. I'm good in math, but I don't like memorizing text. I wonder how I ever learned the times tables—oh yeah, Mom and the flash cards. How could I forget? We're all dressed up and waiting for Mom to come out of the bedroom.

"We've got to go, Henri," Dad says.

"I'm coming," Mom says as she walks out of the bedroom.

"Wow," Dad says. Mom's got a dress on and high heels with her hair up and her lipstick on.

She looks so beautiful. I can't believe she's my Mom. Dad says wow again and Mom blushes.

"What this old dress?" Mom says like a young girl.

We laugh and Dad tells Donna and me to get downstairs and see Mrs. Segal. She wants to see how we look. I'm more than happy to see Mary Anne. I've got a suit on today. Aunt Ruth and Uncle Al bought me the suit and Donna a dress. They like to buy us clothes for special occasions.

Dad runs ahead of us down the front steps to drive the car to the front of the house. Donna and I follow him down the stairs and knock on Mrs. Segal door. She opens the door and invites us in. Mrs. Segal says I look handsome and Donna's so pretty. The girls make a fuss about Donna. Mary Anne doesn't notice me. Rita smiles at me. Wait till they see Mom who I hear just starting down the stairs. Suddenly there's a terrible bang in the stairwell and Mrs. Segal runs past us.

She yells out the door to Dad, "Rich get in here; Henri fell down the stairs."

I run to the door to the entry way and see Mom folded up on the floor between the end of the stairs and the wall. She's not talking; her eyes are closed. I turn to stop Donna from coming any closer. Dad comes in the door from the porch. He looks so scared.

"Henri, Henri! Are you okay?"

Mom doesn't say a word; she doesn't move. Mr. Segal is on the phone talking to the police. He tells Dad an ambulance is coming.

"Ray, can you take the kids to church?" Dad says to Mr. Segal.

"I will," he replies.

"Okay, kids," Dad says. "Mom's going to be okay."

Mr. Segal wants us to follow him to the back door. What do I do? I don't want to go.

"Is my Ma alive?"

Mr. Segal opens the back door of his car. He doesn't answer my question. He won't even look at us. Donna and I get in the car.

CHAPTER 25

The Sym-phony

~⁀

I can't hear anything the minister is saying—I don't care right now! All I want is for Mom to be okay. Dear God, please make Mom okay. What else can I say to make Him hear me? I'm never sure He's listening. Mom says not to worry; everything's for the good in His time and in His way. All things turn out for the best even if we don't understand. Right now I want Mom to be okay. Donna seems all right. She said she saw Mom open her eyes before we left. I didn't see it. I hope she's right. It's almost time for me to say my verses—I can't remember anything right now—I can't believe we're here. Dear God, please make Mom all right …

"Now we're going to hear from the graduating class. Each of the students has memorized verses from the New Testament." The minister gets my attention.

Oh no, here we go. I'm going to make a fool of myself. No one's said anything about Mom. I know they know it, I heard Aunt Leota tell Aunt Net. At least I'm last, Fred's first.

"And our first graduate is Fredrick."

Fred's going to make us all look bad. He had his verses memorized in minutes; I've been at it all week. I know Fred's smart, but that's crazy. Why's it so easy for him? How did Mom fall down the stairs? I've only fallen down stairs once and I walk on crutches. I wish somebody would stop this and tell Donna and me we can leave now!

"Richard." My name, is it my turn?

"Fred, is it my turn?"

"Yeah."

Here goes nothing. I hate walking up stairs to recite. My arms get so weak and shake when I'm taking the stairs in front of a lot of people. I'm afraid I'm going to fall. The last thing I want to do is create a scene. If I fall, there'll be a gasp from the audience and everyone in the front and on the pulpit will run to help me. I know they'd do it for anyone, but for me everyone is on the edge of their seat getting ready to respond. I don't like being the cause of discomfort. Shaking like I am doesn't help. I've got to do this; I wish Mom and Dad were here.

~

"Dad, Ma's alright?"

"Your Mom's home for a little while, you can go and see her in the living room. The ambulance is coming soon to take her back to the hospital."

"Why, Dad?"

"Your Mom can't lift her head without passing out, so the doctor wants her in the hospital for a few days."

I see Mom lying on the couch covered with a blanket. Donna and I walk over to her as quietly as we can. I'm afraid she'll pass out again if we move too quickly and I don't want to see that.

Mom gives us a little smile. "Hi, kids. I'm okay."

Her eyes look so tired and her voice is so weak; I've never seen Mom like this. I touch her shoulder to see if she's warm. Is she really okay?

"What happened, Ma?"

Dad answers. "Your Mom was carrying a big plate of sandwiches when she was coming down the stairs and caught her high heal in the hem of her dress. She didn't reach out for the banister because she didn't want to drop the sandwiches. She never touched a step after that. Her head hit the door and she got a serious concussion."

"Her head is broken?" I say in alarm.

"It's okay," Dad says. "It's just broken a little; your Mom will be okay."

Mom smiles again and the doorbell rings. It's the ambulance man.

It's been two weeks since Mom's fall and she's much better. Dad's been talking with Mom about his new job. He likes being on the road and it pays almost as much as he was paid at Hamilton. He says there's still lots of work outside the shop, but those days are ending. Dad tells everybody that someday they'll just replace an engine that needs work. I hope it's not soon; Dad doesn't like doing anything else but machine work on cars. Someday I hope I get to do the same work, so I can see why he likes it so much.

Another problem solved this week: I got glasses. Now I've got four legs and four eyes! I can't believe what I've been missing. For so long now, I haven't been able to see the board; I thought there was a problem. Mom and I went to the eye doctor just before she fell. One day I complained in class that I couldn't see the board and the teacher said I needed to get my eyes checked. Well, she was right. Getting my eyes checked wasn't as much fun as I hoped. I didn't like the eye drops and how the drops made it even harder to see. It didn't last long, just a few hours. Now I can see the board.

Tonight we're going to Marianne's house. Dad and Earl are working on Earl's car. Dad said Marianne told him to tell me she got some new records. When we get to Marianne's, she and I usually go to her bedroom and listen to her records. She dances and I watch. She seems to like me, but I'm not sure. She's older than me, so I don't want to make a fool of myself. Actually, I'm not sure what I'd do, I've never held or kissed a girl. Fred has, but he knew the girl wanted him to kiss her. We went to a dance at his school and when we left, he left with a girl and a friend of his left with a girl. They stopped and sat on a bench on the way home. Fred and the other boy kissed the girls. I didn't know what to do. I just stood nearby and watched the traffic.

"Here's the records I got, 'Walk Don't Run,' 'Stay,' and 'Poetry in Motion.' Which one do you want to hear first?"

"How about 'Walk Don't Run?'" Marianne is definitely poetry in motion when she dances to songs like "Walk Don't Run." I can't believe how good she dances. I wish I could dance with her. Sitting here on the floor watching her is okay. She's so beautiful and I love watching her move when she dances. I wonder if Marianne knows how much I like to watch her dance. Watching her, all I can think of is the song "It's Only Make Believe."

If only she wasn't older than me. Marianne interrupts my thoughts, "The next song I'm going to get is 'The Twist.'"

"I love that song," I answer, imagining her dancing to "The Twist."

Mary Jane's my age, but she doesn't know I'm alive and Marianne's older than me. She's got a boyfriend who drives a car, but she and I are friends—good friends. There's got to be an answer to this. She puts on a new record, it's "Donna" by Ritchie Valens. Marianne starts singing, "Oh, Donna, oh, Donna" in my face. Look at that smile— what a tease!

"Okay, you're funny," I say with a laugh. "I'm not my sister!"

"You're definitely not your sister," Marianne says with a look. What does that look mean? Is she flirting with me? I wish I knew what to do.

We're having a school outing this afternoon. The sixth graders are going on school buses to the auditorium to hear the City symphony. That's a funny word, "sym-phony." Anybody who likes that music sure is a phony. "Mack the Knife" and "Dream Lover," those're songs. We guys are just happy we don't have any school work to do. My buddy Larry and I are going to sit together.

Larry and I are in the same Webelos den. Soon we're going to be Boy Scouts. The Boy Scout uniform is so much better and in Boy Scouts you get to go camping. Aunt Ruth and Uncle Al bought me my uniform for Christmas and Nana and Papa bought me the Boy Scout ring. Mom and Dad bought me a sleeping bag. I'm ready to go. Wait till Mary Jane sees me in my Boy Scout uniform. That'll get her attention.

We've arrived at the auditorium and we have to take the stairs to the balcony, our classes are going to the top floor, the third floor.

"Larry, take this crutch; it'll be faster if I use the railing."

I climb the steps as fast as I can until we run outta stairs.

"Well we didn't hold them up too much, Larry."

"No, you got up the stairs fast."

The symphony seems to last forever. I've been looking at my watch. I want to be sure there's not much time left when we get back to school. If there is, we'll be doing work.

"Larry, I think it's over. We've still got an hour before the end of school, I bet we have to do work when we get back."

"Yeah," Larry answers, clearly disappointed.

At this point, we'd both rather listen to the symphony. Funny how the thought of class work is worse than listening to the symphony. I give Larry my crutch as we start down the stairs, but the other kids are going down a lot faster than they came up. By the beginning of the last flight of stairs there's no one in front of us.

"Rick, we're alone." I think Larry's getting nervous.

We finally make it outside and all the buses are gone. Our bus is nowhere in sight.

"Where's our bus?" Larry says, sounding a little scared.

"I think they left us."

CHAPTER 26

The Man

It feels so weird. We're standing in front of the auditorium alone. I have no idear how we're gonna get home. Auto Gear's not too far away, but Dad doesn't work there anymore. Maybe we should go see John? Then I see our solution.

"Hey, Larry, there's a policeman; he'll help us."

We run over to the policeman and explain what happened. He tells us he and his partner will take us back to school and he wants our phone numbers. It takes a while, but he finally gets off the radio and tells us they're taking us home. Larry and I smile at each other, no school work for us after all and we get to ride in a police car. What an end to this day! Since Larry and I did so good, I think I'll ask Mom if he and I can go downtown on a bus and see a movie.

Larry and I just got on the bus to go to the movies! Mom and Donna are home alone. Dad's out at the Boy Scout camp getting his Order of the Arrow. He trains new Cub Scout leaders and Dad wants to get the award. He said it's an honor. It's not easy to get. He stayed out last night and tonight alone in the woods. It's one of the things he has to do to get it; he has to survive in the woods for two days and two nights. I don't think he'll have any trouble. He's using my sleeping bag. I haven't even gotten to use it yet. It rained last night. No, it poured. I wonder if it rained where Dad is.

"Larry, this is our stop."

Larry reaches up and pulls on the cord. The bus driver starts to slow down. Wow, here we are in the City all by ourselves. I can't believe it. We've got a bus token for the return trip and money for lunch and the movie. There are so many people and so many cars.

"Rick, where do you want to get lunch?"

"There's a diner right over there."

The diner's almost next to the theater. I feel so grownup.

"Isn't this great?" I say as we sit down at a little table by the window.

"Yeah, what are you going to order for lunch?"

"A BLT," I say like I do it every day. "What're you gonna get?"

"A hamburg," Larry responds not looking up from the menu.

We order cokes and our sandwiches and eat slowly watching the people walk by the window. Everybody looks so busy. The City is exciting. We finally finish; it's only a half an hour before the movie starts.

"Okay, Larry, I've got 35 cents, no candy for me."

"Hey," Larry says. "I've only got 30 cents.

"Whaddya mean, Larry? You need 35 cents to get in the movie."

Larry checks his pockets, goes back in the diner and looks on the floor, and I look around the sidewalk. No nickel.

"Whaddya gonna do?" I ask Larry, feeling like we've really screwed up.

How could we have spent too much? We calculated it carefully; I go back over the numbers.

"Larry, they either didn't give you back the right change, or you dropped a nickel."

Larry looks down at the money in his hand and then he looks at me with a grin on his face.

"The barber shop across the street, the barber's a friend of my dad's. I'll ask him for a nickel.

Larry checks the traffic and works his way across the busy street. I stand in front of the theater feeling a little stupid; we can't even get this right. I see a Lincoln cruising slowly, very close to the curb, and it stops in front of me. Only rich people drive Lincolns. A man gets out. He's tall and wearing a suit. He smiles my way and walks toward me.

"Hi, young man," he says.

"Hi."

"What are you doing?" he asks.

"I'm going to see the movie with my friend."

I think about telling him about the nickel, but before I get to tell him, he asks, "What would you do with 10 dollars?"

"I'd by a model ship or car," I answer without hesitation. Making models is one of my favorite things to do.

With that, he takes out his wallet and gives me 10 dollars, smiles, and starts to walk back to his car.

"Thank you," I holler above the traffic noise.

"Enjoy the movie."

The man gets in the car and waves to me as he merges into the traffic; the excitement is overwhelming. I've never held a $10 bill before. I've barely seen one. Got to get Larry, it's almost time for the movie. I work my way across the street and wave the $10 bill in Larry's face.

"Hey, where'd you get that?" Larry asks

"A man, let's go, we've got nine dollars and 95 cents change."

We have just enough time to get candy and get to our seats as the curtain opens. The movie's great, but I'm preoccupied with thoughts about the model I want. I keep looking in my shirt pocket. I've never had this much money before. Finally, the movie ends and Larry and I leave the theater.

"Where do you want to go?" Larry asks.

"Let's go to Forbes and Wallace." I know they've got great models of cars and ships. We start down the side street to Forbes and a little green Volkswagen pulls up next to us, rolling slowly as we continue to walk. I'm not stopping.

"Hey, guys, you want a ride home?"

I look in the car and it's the guy who gave me the 10 dollars, but now he's driving a Volkswagen Bug and he's not wearing a suit.

"No, thank you," I tell him. "We're gonna buy the model."

"You can buy a model any time," he says. "Let me take you home."

I'm suspicious, a different car and different clothes; he's insisting I wait to buy the model. Mom told me about guys like him. When we lived in the Project, our newspaper boy was taken by a man who did bad things to him. We'll get in the car and there'll be no door handles. He won't bring us home, at least not right away. Larry and I can probably fight him off, but I want that model. We cross the street behind the car. The man stops the car, but we're running as fast as I can. I'm tired of fooling around with him, I've got money to spend.

I got the biggest model I've ever seen. It's an aircraft carrier and it's so big, Larry has to carry it. I can't wait to start making it. We were real careful to avoid that guy. We didn't go into Forbes immediately. We went from store to store and then we left Forbes through a different door.

We catch the bus and head to my house.

"I'm home, Ma. Look what I got!"

"Where'd you get that?" Mom asks suspiciously.

"I got it at Forbes," I say proudly. I relate the entire story to Mom.

"What?" She yells.

I guess I told her too much. I probably should have left out the part about the Volkswagen. I thought she'd be impressed that Larry and I could get away from the guy, but Mom's not comforted by our ability to get home safely.

"I'm calling your Uncle Jerry to come and get us; your father's not home tonight, so we're not staying here. We're staying at Aunt Leota's and that model's going in the trash."

I'd given the change to Mom as an expression of good will, so I'm even out that.

Uncle Jerry's here in his new red Falcon. I'm glad we're going to Fred's, but I'm gonna miss that model. I love making them, especially cars. I love cars, just like Dad.

As we turn onto Aunt Leota's street, I ask Mom a question, "Can Fred and I go to the hill with the wagon?"

"No," Mom says. "The man might still be following us."

I wake up at Fred's house listening to the wind and rain. It's been raining all night. I hear Dad talking downstairs; he's back from the Boy Scout camp and he came to Aunt Leota's. I want to see Dad. Fred's awake, so he follows me downstairs. I don't see Dad.

"Hi, Ma, where's Dad?"

"He's lying on the couch in the front room."

"How come?"

"He's got a terrible headache," Mom says almost in a whisper.

"How come?" I ask again.

"The weather was terrible at the Boy Scout Reservation. It rained and the wind blew hard all day yesterday and all last night. He couldn't sleep trying to keep his tent up and last night he couldn't start a fire to cook his beans and hot dogs, so he ate the beans cold. When your dad got here he was soaking wet and in such pain.

"Did Dad get the Order of the Arrow?"

"Yes he completed the requirements for the award."

"Can I see Dad?"

"Why don't you wait till he gets some sleep? Let's have breakfast."

Fred and I have English muffins, but it was a close one. Fred complained because Mom didn't buy fork cut English muffins. He can really complain over some of the silliest things. Fred was standing in front of the open cellar door and for a moment I thought Mom was going to push him down the stairs. She was so mad.

After we finish breakfast, Dad comes into the kitchen. He doesn't look good. He looks grey, his eyes are half closed, and his voice is weak. I can tell his head hurts. It must be his blood pressure again.

CHAPTER 27
Crushed Cookies

~⌐

Schools out, summers here, and another trip to see Dr. Derby—it's become a tradition. As the elevator climbs to the second floor, I wonder what's planned for this summer. Mom and I wait for over an hour and finally Martha tells us to go into the examination room. We enter the room at the same time Dr. Derby walks in from his office with my folder in his hand.

"Well Ricky, how's school?" Dr. Derby asks.

Schools always first on his mind, he never asks, how's therapy? I guess I don't have a very positive answer for either question. I see no gain with therapy and I'm doing okay in school but not as good as everyone says I can do. Therapy, school, and girls; they're all not going so good. I wonder if they're somehow related.

"School's good, Dr. Derby," I answer looking at Mom because I've learned over the years that the question's for both of us.

"He's getting too many C's," Mom answers.

Dr. Derby frowns and shakes his head as he writes in my file. We ought to put this on tape and play it back when we come in, it's always the same.

"Ricky, we're going to put your left leg in a cast for a month," Dr. Derby says.

All I can think of is it's another month of scratching. I wish I had a vote here.

Turning to Mom, he continues, "I want to stretch the hamstrings in the back of Ricky's leg. When the cast comes off, he will need intensive therapy for the rest of the summer to see if his left leg will straighten, so he can lock his knee."

I can't put a lot of weight on my left leg. It's still not strong enough to hold me for very long.

"I also want to put a half inch lift on his right shoe. We've been talking about this for a while, I think the time has come."

First I've got two different size shoes and now I'm gonna have a thicker sole and heal on my right shoe. That won't be too obvious!

"I'll see you at the hospital a week from this Monday at 9 o'clock? Get the lift done on his right shoe, so he has the lift when he gets the cast."

"That would be fine," Mom says with a smile.

We leave and get on the elevator, I can see Mom's expression has changed, she's not very happy.

"I guess we better go get you a pair of shoes. You've only got one pair and you can't wear your shoe with the lift until you get the cast. I don't know where we're going to get the money for this. He must think we're made of money." Mom says with a combination of disgust and anger. I know Mom doesn't mean it. She's not mad, she's frustrated.

On the appointed Monday morning, we walk to the hospital. Jack and Dr. Derby are waiting for us. I take off my pants, left shoe, and sock and get up on the table. Jack takes a number of rolls of plaster and a roll of cotton wrap. He wraps my leg from my toes to my thigh with the cotton. That's gonna be the itchy layer between my leg and the plaster. After the cotton wrap is done, Jack picks up the first roll of plaster and dips it in a bowl of hot water. Jack lifts the roll out of the water and lets the excess water drip back into the bowl. Now he's pulling the end away from the roll and wraps my leg starting at my toes. He'll use many rolls of plaster to make the cast. As Jack gets past my calf and starts wrapping my knee, Dr. Derby asks Jack to put a few extra wraps around my knee. When Jack finishes, Dr. Derby presses down on my left knee until the back of the cast touches the table. He holds the cast down while it dries. As it's drying it warms up. On a hot summer day it just starts the process of itching that much sooner. I wish we did this in the winter.

I can walk with this cast, so Mom and I are going to walk back to Aunt Ruth's and wait for Dad to pick us up tonight. Mom thinks it's too far for me to walk home with the cast. My leg hurts as it usually does when it's forced straight, but this time it's going to stay that way for a month. I hope it doesn't take long for the pain to go away. I must look like a train wreck: crutches, a cast on one leg and a lift on my right shoe.

"Ricky, what are you doing?" Mom asks as if she doesn't know.

"I'm scratching, Ma!"

I've got the knitting needle almost buried in the cast and I'm squirming in agony; what I don't need is the question. The cotton wrap doesn't last long once I start pushing the knitting needle down to scratch.

"I don't want you to cut yourself with that needle," Mom scolds.

I couldn't agree more. At this point a hack saw or cleaver would do a better job. Most of the itches are just a fingertip further away. I've got an itch behind my knee that I just can't quite reach and one I don't even want to talk about just above my ankle. When I give up with the needle I pound the cast over the itches, anything to move the cast against the itch.

"Ma, this is driving me crazy."

"I know," Mom says, "just a few more days."

Mom's sincere, but it doesn't help. We've barely been out of the house for the past month. I'm back to not being able to do stairs very easily, so it's easier to stay home. Just two more days and the cast comes off. The first two days with the cast were uncomfortable to say the least. The back of my knee felt like the skin would tear at any moment. I had about a week of pain and numbness in my leg, then the itching started. The scenario's always the same, the itch starts on the bottom of my foot. It's a stretch, but I can reach it and then it moves to my thigh. Once I've relieved those, it moves behind my knee. I know that I could unwind a clothes hanger, straighten it out, and reach the itch, but I'd scratch myself and an infection would be worse. I bang on the cast behind the knee and then the itch starts just above my ankle. It seems that Mom and Dad have moved all the tools that I might use to hit the cast harder. If only I could have a few minutes with a hammer.

Finally, the day has arrived. I'm in the cast room. There're two nuns in the room who offer me cookies; I take two handfuls. I thought it was funny, two handfuls and it's not even lunch time. The nuns must think it's funny too because they smiled. I've decided not to eat any of the cookies until the cast is off. I'm gonna enjoy them when Jack's done. Jack's standing there with the saw in his hand. He's ready and I couldn't be more anxious. Jack takes his usual route starting at my big toe. He grinds through the thick cast around my ankle and moves quickly up the calf. When he reaches the knee he's slowed again by the thick cast that held my knee straight for the past month. He finally cuts through the mass at my knee and starts up my inner thigh when it happens.

There's a pain that feels like Jack just cut my leg off mid-thigh. The cookies in my hand are crumbs all over me, the table, and the floor. I've crushed both handfuls. I know he cut a hole in my thigh. Where's the blood?

"I'm sorry, Ricky; the blade's hot."

Hot, he never said anything about hot. Oh! That hurts so much.

"Just a little more, Ricky."

I look at him hoping he'll stop and give me a moment to recover and let the blade cool.

"Just a little more, I won't burn you again."

I squeeze the crumbs in my hand into powder as Jack finishes the cut. Jack pulls the cast apart at the top and there it is . . . a burn. It's about an inch long, the skin is red and raised like a long, thin, red bubble. Suddenly I feel the air hit my skin. It feels so cool. Jack finishes cutting the other side and I get new cookies, a leg wash, and time to scratch.

Now I have to wear the new shoes with the lift and exercise more than ever. Up and down stairs, back and forth between the parallel bars, more stretching of my left leg. This goes on all summer, but as school gets closer to starting, it's obvious the leg just won't stay straight. The lift is becoming a serious problem as the toe of my right shoe jams against the ground with every step. I don't have enough strength in my right hip to swing my right leg out. I can only swing it straight forward when I take a step. Unless I can lift myself with my left leg and foot, my right shoe can't swing through. Dr. Derby decides to have the lift removed from my shoe and he says we'll try another method to straighten that leg when I'm older. I wonder what he's planning, I'm curious, but I think I'll wait to find out.

Tomorrow's the first day of junior high and I'm sick. Seems like I'm always sick when I get excited about something. I run a fever every Christmas Eve, and now, the night before the first day of junior high, I'm excited about going and I'm running a fever.

"It's 100," Mom says, sounding a little exasperated.

Fifth and sixth grade were the first years I'd not been sick a lot and here it is the night before my first day of seventh grade and I'm running a fever. I hope it's not gonna be another year of being sick. It shouldn't be, I've had everything a kid can get including polio, mumps, measles, German measles, chickenpox, croup, ear aches, and a slew of fevers for no apparent reason. Oh yeah, I almost forgot pneumonia and the flu. The worst of the bunch is the flu. I hate throwing up. I always feel like my insides are coming out.

"I guess you're not going to school tomorrow," Mom says. "If you don't run a fever tomorrow, you can go to school the next day."

What a pain. I can't wait to go to junior high where we change rooms for every class and take shop. Wood shop's the first shop class. I want to make a three legged stool. Dad says I'll learn about using tools and machines. I can't wait—I guess I'm gonna have to wait.

CHAPTER 28

Junior High

~⌐

Day two of school and I'm on my way. It's a longer walk, but it will be good exercise.

"Use that left leg!" Mom yells from the porch as I walk down the sidewalk. Day two of school and my first—not a good start. I'll catch up. I've done it enough.

I'm in homeroom and there're a lot of new kids from other elementary schools. The kid next to me looks like he owns the place. He's sitting like he's in a lounge chair with his arms crossed and a big smile on his face. I'm not sure he combed his hair this morning. He looks like he rolled out of bed, pulled on his clothes, and came to school.

He looks at me and says, "I'm Paul, what's your name?"

"Rick."

"Are you Rick the stick?" Paul asks.

"Stick? Oh yeah, no Rick Willett." Can't hide these crutches!

"What's with the sticks?" Paul questions looking like he's never seen crutches before.

"I had polio."

Paul sits up straight in his chair, leans toward me, and asks, "Is that why you weren't here yesterday?"

I explain to him that I had polio at age two and no, I had a fever Sunday night, so my Mom kept me home.

"What, you do everything your mom tells you?" Paul asks with a scowl.

I'm not sure what to say. I thought everybody does what their mom tells them to do, but it's apparent I better not say that to Paul. He's different, I like him.

"I'm going to tell you right now Rick, I'm the champion ranker, so don't even try to rank on me." I smile, but I haven't a clue what rank means. I better ask Mom before Paul finds out I don't understand.

Our homeroom teacher has us stand up and say the pledge of allegiance, then he calls me up to his desk to pick up some paperwork for Mom. Suddenly, the bell rings and everybody jumps out of their seats.

I ask Paul, "Where're the shops?"

"Shops?" Paul says with his now familiar scowl.

"Yeah, like wood shop."

"What, you need your sticks fixed?" Paul shoots back.

Before he can say anything else I explain that wood shop's my first class. As we walk into the hallway, Paul points to the stairs and says the shops are downstairs.

"Hey, I'll see ya later," Paul says as he strolls off in another direction.

Then I realize who Paul reminds me of, the boy Pinocchio met on Pleasure Island.

I make my way down the stairs and see Larry on his way to another shop.

"Hey, Rick, wait for me after school out front. I need to talk to you about the dance."

I take a seat in wood shop on a wooden bench with everyone else. I wonder what Larry was talking about, a dance? The teacher, Mr. Johnson takes attendance and tells us to get to work. I see everybody walk in a room adjoining the shop and selecting pieces of wood. I eye a board about eight inches wide and four feet long. It looks perfect for the seat of my three legged stool. All I have to do is get a saw and cut off a triangular piece from one end. Some of the kids are standing over by the table saw with Mr. Johnson and others are at the tables lining up pieces of wood side by side. I put the board in a vice at the corner of one of the tables, get a saw from an open tool cupboard, and start cutting.

I get about half way through the board when I hear a loud, "What're you doing?"

It's Mr. Johnson and he's looking right at me. Everyone stops working and now the entire class is looking at me. I look at Mr. Johnson and explain the need for a triangular piece of wood for my stool.

"What?" Mr. Johnson says in a loud voice. "Look what you did to my only piece of cherry."

I'm confused, what doesn't he understand? Then I see a look of recognition come across Mr. Johnson's face.

He says, "You were absent yesterday, weren't you?"

"Yes," I say, still confused.

Mr. Johnson explains to me that everyone is making the same project. A cutting board made of nine pieces of wood one inch square and 12 inches long. He directs me to the wood storage and shows me light and dark pieces of oak that I can select from and he'll cut on the table saw. He finishes telling me that I'll glue the nine pieces together, clamp them, and let them dry until we return Friday. Mr. Johnson takes his piece of cherry wood out of the vice. A look of extreme sorrow spreads across his face. I start selecting pieces of light and dark oak. First class and I'm already screwing up.

By the time I get outta the building, Larry's waiting for me.

"So what were you talking about this morning, a dance?"

"Did you know they have a rock and roll dance here every Friday night during the school year?" he says with more excitement than I would expect from Larry, considering the subject.

"I didn't know you like to dance."

"How could you not like to dance? You get to dance with a girl," Larry whispers excitedly.

"I didn't say I don't like to dance," I tell him.

This is a side of Larry I've never seen before. All the time we've hung out and he's never mentioned girls. Actually, I only hang out with Larry once and a while. He's usually off with his other friends on their bikes. I don't think his friends know this about Larry either. All the boys I know think girls are creepy. It's looks like Larry and I have something very important in common. It's been a while since I square danced in fifth grade. I've never done any other type of dancing. I wonder if I can.

"When's the first dance?" I ask.

"This Friday night at 6:30 here in the gym." Larry's excitement hasn't wavered.

I have to admit, I'm as excited as Larry is; I'm just not willing to let him know. Got to bring him down a level, he could embarrass us both at the dance if he stays this way.

"You know you have to ask the girls to dance, don't you?" I ask. "It's not like fifth grade square dancing where Mrs. Jackson paired me with a girl."

"Yeah, I didn't think about that," Larry says with a little concern coming across his face.

That might have done it, but I've got to be careful. I don't want Larry to not go; I just don't want him popping off like fireworks. We start home and Larry's still got a grin on his face.

I've never seen him like this. Now if I can just contain my excitement. Holding a girl again, there's nothing like that.

CHAPTER 29

The Fight

It's Thursday lunch and there's Larry. He's still got that grin. I grab a tray and silverware and join him in line.

"So, Larry, have you heard anybody talking about going to the dance?"

"Yeah, some eighth grade girls were talking about it at the lockers and they seemed excited."

I take a plate from the lunch lady. Today is hamburg gravy on mashed potatoes with green beans, one of my favorites. I grab a brownie, milk, pay for my lunch, and follow Larry to a table. In elementary school I brought lunch, but I'm gonna buy lunch from now on. Only two days buying lunch and I've already become an expert at carrying my tray. I can walk without using my right hand by holding my crutch against my side with my upper arm and swinging the crutch forward with my shoulder. It's a little challenging having to balance the contents of my lunch on a tray, but I can do it.

"Hey, Rick the stick." I don't have to turn around; I know its Paul.

"Hey, Paul."

Paul sits next to me before I can offer him a seat. I notice he's got two brownies.

"How'd you get two brownies?" I ask.

"Easy, just slide one off a plate on top of another when the lunch lady looks away and nobody's the wiser."

"Didn't the checkout lady see it?"

"I put one in my pocket until I paid," Paul informs me and Larry.

Larry and I look at each other. I know we're thinking the same thing. No way—we'd get caught for sure and darned if we'd put food in our pocket. One of Paul's brownies looks like half of it's still in his pocket. It seems he doesn't mind.

Larry and I talk about where we should meet to walk to the dance and he decides he wants to stop at my house. I realize I didn't ask Paul if he was going.

"Paul, you goin to the dance tomorrow night?" I ask, half assuming he'd say no.

"Dance shmance, that's for creeps," Paul enlightens us. "If I want a girl, I don't need no dance."

I wonder for a moment what Paul means by *if I want a girl*. I'm never too sure what he means by some of his comments. He's 13, stayed back once, so he might have more experience with girls than Larry and me. We're 11. Larry's 12 in November and I've got till December. I decide to change the subject and remind Larry we go to our first Boy Scout meeting next Wednesday. I half do it to see what Paul's reaction is and he doesn't disappoint me.

You guys are Boy Scouts too?" Paul says with disgust. "You guys are really scaring me!"

I decide to retaliate with, "You can be a real difficult."

"I'm rubber, you're glue and whatever you say bounces off of me and sticks to you," Paul retorts. "I told you not to try to rank on me, I'm too good at it."

He's right; I forgot to ask Mom about ranking, but now I think I'm getting the idear. At the end of the day, as Larry and I leave school we catch up to Paul who looks like he's checking what's in every yard we walk by.

Two policemen in a police car drive by us at the same time and Paul yells, "Pigs."

Larry looks at Paul and they both start to run. I'm looking at the policemen who look in our direction and come to an immediate stop.

I look around and Larry and Paul have stopped running. Larry looks scared, he's staring at the police car. Paul looks shocked, he's looking at me. I think he forgot I can't run. Of course, I'm surprised they actually stopped. They didn't have to. I expect the policemen to get out and handcuff us and bring us back to the station for assaulting them, but they just scold us. They don't even ask who said pig.

Paul makes the last comment as the police car drives away. "Boy that was close!" He snickers, shakes his head, and waves at us as he walks away.

It takes me some time, but I finally collect enough put downs or ranks as Paul calls em, like "your mother" or "your ugly sister" to keep up with him. It's something that requires verbal skill and quick thinking. There actually seems to be a rule to the ranks. You don't want to say anything that might offend and new ones always help. It took me a while because I thought the comments were degrading to mothers, sisters, and other family members, but I finally realized it was just sparring. We don't do it to hurt or insult each other, but you have to be careful.

I had a little problem earlier today with a kid in art class. Our school is predominately white with some students of other races. This kid's like John at Auto Gear, but unlike John he doesn't have much to say to anyone. I was using some paints and he wanted one and just took it. Now, looking back, I was probably being a little too possessive and he probably should have asked if I was gonna use that color, but I was the one who reacted.

When he took the paint, I said, "Hey."

He said, "What do you mean, hey."

"I was gonna use that color." I was, but not immediately.

He said something like, "Who, you and your ugly sister?"

I couldn't let it pass, so I said, "No, me and your mother."

I knew immediately it was inappropriate. We weren't friends. What I said was fighting words. I won the war of words, but now it would have to move up to the next level.

I was mad enough not to care when he said, "I'll see you after school!"

I said, "I'll be waiting for you out front." I should have begged for forgiveness, but at that point I was convinced I could beat him to a pulp.

That happened at second period so I had all day to think about it. I felt confident: we were the same size, I was probably stronger, and I had my crutches. As the day wore on, I realized that he might be a little more agile than me and he might actually know how to fight. At lunch I told Larry and Paul about the fight and asked them to be seconds. Seconds is a standard practice for fights. You bring along a couple of friends to make sure the fight's fair and to drag you off if you lose. I liked the idear of having them there, but by last class I was having trouble looking forward to the bell.

Finally, the bell rings and I make my way to the front of the school. Larry and Paul are waiting at the bottom of the stairs and I walk down to join them. I'm still feeling somewhat confident, but seeing my opponent and his seconds doesn't bring on the rush of anger I was hoping for. We walk up to each other and all I can think is, how do you actually start a fight, when suddenly he, his name is Sam, raises his open hand offering to shake mine.

"I'm not going to fight you."

I'm shocked. He doesn't seem like the kind of kid who would back down from a fight. There had to be another reason, but I'm not gonna ask what it is. It takes me a moment.

I finally say, "Okay." I raise my hand, grasp his, and shake.

We end the shake and I turn around and see the relief on Larry and Paul's faces. I tell them what I think, that Sam backed down because he didn't want to hurt me. I appreciate the pats on my back they give me. They treat me like a winner. I didn't stand a chance.

Sam gave me the chance to reconsider. I have to admit, I think he's a better man than me. I walk home hearing the song "Mack the Knife" by Bobby Darin in my head. I wish I could be as cool as Bobby Darin.

The Dance

⁓

There's a knock at the back door. It's Larry.

"You ready to go? Oh hi, Mrs. Willett," he blurts out obviously excited.

"Hi, Larry," Mom responds.

"Yeah, I'm ready, let's go."

Now I'm excited and step out the door saying, "By, Ma." I put my crutches down to the first step, but for the first time in my life I've got too much forward momentum. Before I know it I'm airborne headed for the wall. Our back steps go down four steps and then the steps curve in a semi-circle and go straight again. I hit the wall half way around the curve with my left shoulder. Like Mom's fall down the front steps, I never touch a step. I'm lying against the wall on my back with my head down the stairs looking back at Larry who looks like the floor just fell beneath him. His eyes are open so wide I can see more white than blue.

"Hey, that was fun," I say as I grab the railing and pull myself up. I grab a crutch and start down the stairs. I kick the other crutch the rest of the way down the stairs, retrieve it, and turn around to find nobody there.

"Are you okay?" I hear Mom say.

"Yeah, I'm fine."

Larry's not said a word. I hear him finally take his first step. He comes around the corner looking like he's seeing a ghost.

"Are you sure you're okay?" he says.

"Come on," I tell him. "Let's get there before all the girls are taken."

Larry's shock changes to a smile and we both laugh. I think it's funny, but I think Larry's just relieved. The fall takes the excitement down a notch. We walk toward school speculating who might be at the dance. I have one major disappointment—I know Mary Jane's not going.

We're finally in the door and what a gymnasium! This is a big school and we have a gigantic gym. I've never been in here because I don't take gym. The gym has block walls painted light green and a wood floor. There must be 50 kids or more here. The lighting is low and the music is loud. They're playing "Good Timing." A group of kids, mostly girls, are doing the bop. Oh, I wish I could bop. I'll waltz when they play one, if a girl says yes. The song has ended and they're playing "Handyman," another one by Jimmy Jones. I can't believe it, two hours of music like this, wow!

"Larry, can you believe it?" I yell above the music. Now who's excited? I can barely contain myself.

We walk around looking for somebody we know and then I see her. A girl with long blond hair who's so tiny and beautiful, I can't believe my eyes. I'm small, but she's smaller than me. I've never seen her before.

"Larry, look over there," I say pulling on his arm.

"That's Micky Asher," Larry says, like she's just another girl.

"How do you know her?"

"She's in my English class; she's really nice. That's her friend Tania next to her," Larry says acting so cool.

Micky looks like she barely comes up to my chin. Tania's taller, taller than me by a couple of inches. She's got dark hair and very pretty too, but Micky, she's like no other girl here.

"Larry, can you introduce me?" I ask.

"Okay," Larry says walking toward them.

I'm not sure whether to grab him and stop him or follow. I'm not sure I'm ready. Too late, he's outta my reach. I follow.

"Hi, Micky. Hi, Tania." The girls smile. That's a good sign.

"This is my friend, Rick," he says pointing at me.

They both smile and say hi.

I can't believe it. They actually seem interested in talking to us. "Itsy Bitsy Teenie Weenie Yellow Polka Dot Bikini" is playing. Oh, I don't even want to think about Micky and—no, put that outta my mind. Nobody's dancing to this one. We stand and talk; there're no seats. I guess they want us to dance, not sit. Micky and Tania are so nice and easy to talk to. I'm in love. I've never met a girl so easy to talk to. I can't believe she's actually talking to me. "Let the Little Girl Dance" is playing; Micky and Tania walk to the center of the gym and dance. Larry and I watch.

I can see Tommy White looking over at them too. I'm not sure I like him. At recess in elementary school he was always mad when we played soccer baseball. If he had a bad kick and got out, he would sulk all the way back from first base. He never took losing very well. The song's over and here come the girls and Tommy—oh boy.

"Hi, Rick. Hi, Larry," Tommy says.

"Hi, Tommy," we echo.

I know he wants to meet the girls. Larry and I don't have much else to say to him; he finally introduces himself. I'd hoped he wouldn't. The girls say hi but wander off to talk with their friends. Finally, a waltz, "I Want To Be Wanted." This is perfect. I walk over to Micky and ask her if she wants to dance. To my surprise she says yes. For a moment my body goes limp. I'm afraid to move, but I've got to do something with one of the crutches. Okay let's do it. I take a couple of steps to the wall and lean a crutch against it. Micky and I walk out to the dance area and I put my left arm around Micky's neck and rest my hand on her shoulder. She's just the right size. I need to lean on her just a little bit; my left leg isn't quite strong enough yet. She smells so good. She's so soft. I don't know how to explain it; she actually smells soft. I hope I don't step on her feet. She has her arms around me. I've never danced this close to a girl. I want the song to last forever, but my left leg and butt are getting tired. The song ends too soon—but just soon enough.

It's 9 o'clock and they're playing the last song, "Sea of Love." Micky says yes and we finish the night dancing together. It's over, the lights come up, what a night! Larry and I say good night to the girls. We see some of the guys from elementary school and walk outside with them. They're not excited about dancing. They all stood in a corner talking all night. I don't know if they're afraid to ask or afraid to dance, a little of both I guess.

Nobody else waltzed with Micky. I expected one of the eighth graders to ask her to dance, but they didn't even seem to notice her. They gotta be blind, but that's okay. When we get outside, Micky and her friends are ahead of us. I can't wait till next Friday. Larry and I walk home silent in our thoughts. All I can smell is Micky's hair. It smelled so clean, so sweet. I hope she likes the smell of Brylcreem; all us guys use it to keep our hair in place. I wonder if she likes me.

"Larry, do you think Micky likes me?"

"I suppose."

He doesn't sound convincing. I decide not to pursue it. Larry doesn't know any better than I do.

"Hey, Larry, want to come over tomorrow?" He's never come over to visit. We hang out but only when we're going someplace and that's not too often.

"No, I'm going riding with the guys."

"Okay."

I wish I could figure out a way to ride a bike.

We're in front of my house. Larry turns and starts to run, saying, "Hey, I'll see you Monday at school."

"Yeah, I'll see you then," I answer, hoping I didn't sound too disappointed.

What a weekend it would be if Larry came over. Maybe we'll go to Fred's on Sunday.

～♪

I'm awake. I'm sweating, not sure where I am. I had the building dream. It's always the same; I'm looking up through a window at the building. I think I'm lying down in a car or truck. Then we start to move away very slowly and I can see more of the building and then I wake up. I always wake up with this same lonely feeling. I'm not scared, I feel alone, very alone. I'm in my bed, it was just a dream, but I can't shake the feeling.

Now I can't sleep. What a night! I don't think I'll have another one like this. Meeting Micky and dancing with her, it's more than I could have ever expected. I just wish I could bop, but that's okay. Not much I can do to change it. Think I'll read. I'm almost done with Tom Sawyer. I love his carefree life. Now where's the flashlight? Here it is. I hope the batteries last, just about 20 pages left, two more chapters. Got to see if Tom and Huck get out of trouble. What a night tonight—I hope they just get better.

～♪

We've been in school for just over a month now and here I am in math class waiting for Mr. Robinson to hand out our graded first exam. I'm excited—it was so easy. Here's mine, a zero! What's this say? See me after class? I didn't get a zero. These are all correct. Okay, he's going over it. There's no way I got these all wrong.

"Okay class, on number one the answer is x equals 15 and this is how you get that answer."

Yeah that's what I got. Mr. Robinson covers all the questions and I got them all correct. Finally, it's the end of the class and I walk up to Mr. Robinson very confused.

"Mr. Robinson, you marked all my answers wrong and I got them all correct," I tell him being very careful not to offend him.

"That's right and you couldn't have gotten them correct," Mr. Robinson says with an air of authority.

"But I did, the answers are right here," I respond again being very respectful, but I'm exasperated.

"There's no way you could have solved those problems without doing the work," Mr. Robison says, now a little angry.

"But, Mr. Robison, I can get all these answers without doing them; I can do them in my head," I respond not backing down.

"Impossible," Mr. Robinson insists, "you must have cheated."

"Cheated?" I almost yell, now insulted.

I stand there knowing the logic makes no sense to Mr. Robinson. No one around me got a 100, so how did I cheat? I'm not gonna insult Mr. Robinson, I'll talk to Mom about this. I rush home and practically run up the stairs.

"Ma," I yell as I crash through the back door.

"Yes, you don't need to yell," Mom scolds from the living room.

Mom's ironing and watching Art Linkletter. I tell Mom what happened and the error of Mr. Robinson's logic. I insist Mom will have to go to school and see Mr. Robinson. Mom looks at my paper and without a word calls the school. She's talking to Mr. Perry, the principal.

"What did Mr. Perry say, Ma?"

"He said I can come tomorrow after school and talk with Mr. Robinson."

I have math last period, so I'll wait for Mom.

CHAPTER 31

A Blister

At the end of math class, I can see Mom waiting outside the classroom. Just before the bell rings, Mr. Robinson asks me to wait in the hall while he talks to Mom. The bell rings and I get up and walk into the hall.

"Ma, Mr. Robison wants me to wait for you out here," I say quietly.

"Okay," Mom says.

Mr. Robinson is right behind me and introduces himself to Mom. They go into the room together and Mr. Robinson closes the door. I can still see them through the window in the door. At first I can't hear them talking, but after a few minutes I can hear Mom; she's raised her voice a little. I can't hear what she's saying, but I know she must be a little angry. I don't hear them now; it's quiet again. The door suddenly opens and it makes me jump. I was concentrating so hard trying to hear that I had stopped looking through the window. The noise of the knob turning startled me. Mr. Robinson steps out the door and glares at me.

"Ricky, come in," he orders me.

I stand up straight and walk to the door. Mom doesn't have any expression that I can read. I step in the room and Mr. Robinson closes the door behind us. He walks to his desk and sits down. I walk to his desk. Mom is sitting in the chair on the other side of Mr. Robinson's desk.

Mr. Robinson says, "Ricky, I'm going to let you take another test just like this one and if you can answer the questions correctly in the same manner that you did on this test, I'll agree that you didn't cheat and give you a 100."

I hesitate for a moment. I had explained to Mom that she needed to tell Mr. Robinson that I couldn't have cheated because I was the only one who got a 100 that I could see, at least everyone around me. If Mom did explain it to Mr. Robinson, obviously the logic didn't convince him, but at least he's willing to let me prove I can get the answers.

After an uncomfortable pause I say, "Thank you." Mom and I leave. Tomorrow's Friday, I have to stay after school and take the test, again.

That night in bed as usual I can't sleep. I can hear Mom telling Dad everything that Mr. Robinson said. He still insisted I cheated somehow.

I hear Mom say, "I almost got out of the chair to throttle him."

Dad laughs and stops. Obviously Mom wasn't laughing.

"Oh don't be so serious about this," Dad says.

"He made me very angry."

"I know," Dad says, "but you got him to let Ricky take the test again."

"Ricky shouldn't have to," Mom retorts. "My son doesn't cheat."

I have to agree with Mom.

"I know," Dad says gently. "His teacher will find that out."

That ends the discussion. I think about Boy Scouts. Larry and I have been going for a month now and it's a lot of fun. We work toward our merit badges and we play games. I couldn't play the last one, but it was so much fun watching. There's four of us new scouts and we've been in initiation all month. This week was our last test and I got out of it. Our Scout Master, Mr. DeAngelo, brought in a long four-by-four and put it between two chairs. He sent the new scouts outside except for Larry. He divided the scouts, except two of the older scouts, into two groups and had each of the two groups stand at the ends of the four-by-four. Mr. DeAngelo put a blindfold on Larry and told him he had to get up on the center of the four-by-four and balance himself with the help of the two older scouts, the two scouts helped Larry up and then they each held a hand. Mr. DeAngelo said the other boys were going to pick up the four-by-four and Larry had to keep his balance.

Mr. DeAngelo told the scouts to lift the four-by-four and they all made a noise like they're lifting. The two scouts holding Larry's hands slowly squatted down. The four-by-four didn't move, but obviously Larry thought it did. He started to flail around and yell. He fell off the four-by-four and Mr. DeAngelo caught him. We all laughed; Larry looked so funny. When Larry took off the blindfold, he looked so scared and we were laughing so hard. Larry had no idear what happened. One of the scouts went outside and got Billy, one of the other new scouts, and Larry got to see what happened.

I let out a chuckle and Mom asks from the living room, "What are you laughing about?"

"Nothing," I answer. Guess I better get to sleep, soon.

I wonder if Micky would go out with me if I ask her or maybe I shouldn't. If she says no, it could end her dancing with me. Think I'll wait a little while. Mr. DeAngelo said we're going camping this winter during Christmas vacation up at the Boy Scout reservation and we're gonna sleep in tents. I hope Mom doesn't spoil it for me. She's bound to say, you'll freeze that leg. Got to wait for the right time to ask her, I'll think about it later. Should I ask Micky to go steady?

Well Mr. Robinson kept his word, it's another test just like the one I took. It takes me less than a half an hour to finish. I'm sitting at the desk right on front of Mr. Robinson. The desk touches Mr. Robinson's, so I just hand the test to him.

Mr. Robinson looks over the test, looks up at me and says, "I'm sorry; you can do the problems without working them out."

I decide not to smile. "Thank you, Mr. Robinson. Did I get them all correct?"

"Yes you did," Mr. Robinson says with a smile. "I guess I taught you well."

"Yes you did." I get up and tell Mr. Robinson to have a great weekend.

I've got to get going; I've got a dance to get ready for.

I leave the school and cross the street. Aunt Ruth lives across the street and I'm staying with her and Uncle Al tonight. Uncle Al's gone to work by now. I'm going to the dance from Aunt Ruth's; I'll meet Larry there

"Hi, Aunt Ruth," I yell as I walk in the door.

"Hi, Ricky, I'm in the living room."

I walk into the living room and see that Aunt Ruth looks very sad. "What's the matter, Aunt Ruth?"

"I'm waiting for a phone call from Uncle Al."

"Is it a bad call?"

"It could be, Ricky, Uncle Al might lose his job."

I realize immediately how bad the phone call might be. Uncle Al has a very good job and often Aunt Ruth and Uncle Al buy Donna and me things that Mom and Dad can't afford. They buy us clothes for Easter and they paid for us all to go to Niagara Falls three years ago. They pay for all the times we've stayed in a cottage in the summer. Aunt Ruth has always been able to shop and not worry about the cost, not like Mom. Mom always worries. I tell Aunt Ruth about the test. She's interested, but I know she's thinking about Uncle Al. I ask her what's happening at Uncle Al's work that he might lose his job.

"They're having a meeting at work because one of the guards didn't do his work right, and the owners of the company think all the guards may be not be doing their work, something to do with not making their rounds around the building. One of the guards figured out a way to fool the punch card system, so it looked like he actually did his job. The owners don't know if they're all doing it or just that man."

The phone rings. Aunt Ruth picks it up and says hello. I don't want to listen, but I can tell she's talking with Uncle Al. She's very quiet. I can see tears forming in her eyes. She says goodbye. I wait for Aunt Ruth to talk; I don't want to ask. I'm afraid to ask.

Finally, she says, "The company is going to let all of their guards go. They can go to work for a company that hires out guards, but it pays minimum wage. We can't live on that."

I leave for the dance feeling guilty about leaving Aunt Ruth. She insisted I go to the dance, but I'm not feeling good about it. Mom's not home tonight because she's been going over to Nana's a lot. Mom just told us she's going because Nana is very sick. I know what it is, its cancer. I heard Mom say it to Dad the other night. Sometimes listening to Mom and Dad at night I learn things I wish I didn't know.

Boy that sure was a short walk to the dance. There's Larry. As we walk into the gym, the first song starts. It's "Teen Angel." Where's Micky? I don't see her.

"Larry, where's Micky, do you see her?" I ask in a panic. "I've got to find her before …"

"I see her," Larry says. "She's over there dancing with Tommy."

I look over—I can't watch—I walk outside. Larry's not far behind me.

"Are you okay?"

"Yeah," I say, trying to sound as unemotional as I can. Inside I feel like somebody just punched me in the stomach. If I had just left Aunt Ruth's one minute earlier. But then, I also wish I had stayed with her.

"You're upset," Larry chides me.

"No I'm not," I insist. "I just don't like Tommy. He can dance all the fast dances he wants with Micky. He couldn't wait to get this chance."

"Then you're upset."

"I'm out here so I don't have to watch, that's all," I insist. The song ends and Larry and I go back in.

The dance is over and Larry and I leave. I got to dance with Micky once. She had to leave early. There was only one more waltz before she left, "Lonely Boy." I just beat Tommy to her. He's gonna be a pest. The last song tonight was "Maybe." I wish Micky stayed until the end. Lonely boy, just what I'm feeling. I'm not one to complain, but lonely describes how I feel so often, especially after the dream about the building. It's nobody's fault and I don't let it get me down, but it's real. Someday it will go away. Someday I'll find a girl of my own. Like in Dad's song, a doll the other fellas cannot steal.

My right leg is killing me. I think I've got another blister at the top of my leg, in the back where my weight rests on the top of my brace. It started this morning on my way to school. It hurt a lot when I got to the dance, but it really hurts now. It's the second one. It must be the extra walking I do now in junior high; I've got to check it at Aunt Ruth's. I have to walk on it until it bursts. That worked last time. I don't want to tell Mom; she'll make me sit until it goes away. I don't have time for that.

"Why are you walking so slow?" Larry asks as we make our way to the sidewalk.

"I think I've got a blister on the back of my leg. It hurts a lot right now. I think it's ready to burst," I tell Larry trying not to sound too wounded. It's about 40 or 50 feet to the sidewalk. I can barely put any weight on the brace, but maybe if I put my weight on it it'll burst before I get to Aunt Ruth's. We walk about 30 feet, slowly. Larry keeps looking back at me. Finally, I feel a lot less pain.

"I think it broke."

"The blister?" Larry asks.

"Yeah, it doesn't hurt as much and I feel something running down the back of my leg. That's what happened last time."

"Yuck," Larry says.

"Yuck nothing," I tell him. "It feels better."

By the time we get to the sidewalk, the pain is almost gone. I say goodbye to Larry and cross the street to Aunt Ruth's. I say hello to Aunt Ruth and head for the bathroom. I take my pants and brace off and I see the blood that ran down my leg, just a little ways. It's dry now. I clean the back of my leg and put my brace and pants back on. I hope this doesn't happen too often.

Aunt Ruth and I wait up for Uncle Al to come home.

When he arrives, Aunt Ruth fixes him a coffee and I wait in the living room while they talk in the kitchen. I know Uncle Al can't be that old. He's older than Dad, but he's got to be only in his 40's. He looks so much older. Papa's older and even he looks younger than Uncle Al. Uncle Al says it's the arthritis. His fingers are swollen and twisted and he walks like he's in pain, but he never complains. He's always got a smile for me. Uncle Al has to walk to take the bus to work. When I see him walking down the street leaning a little like he can't stand up all the way and each step looking like it's a struggle, I don't feel so bad about having polio. I'm young and getting stronger. Uncle Al won't get better.

Tonight he looks and sounds so tired. It's no wonder; Uncle Al snores so loud. Aunt Ruth sleeps in another room even though Uncle Al works all night and he's not home most nights. I don't know how Uncle Al can sleep with the noise. Mom says it's from his injury in the war.

"Ricky, how was the dance tonight?" Uncle Al asks from the kitchen.

I jump up and run to the kitchen. "It was great, Uncle Al," I answer with as much enthusiasm as I can muster. "They played 'The Twist' tonight. It's the first fast dance I can do."

Uncle Al smiles, reaches out, and puts his arm around my waist. He gives me a hug and holds me for a while.

I've got to ask, "Uncle Al, you didn't do anything wrong at work?"

"No I didn't. One of the guards learned how to change the main clock, so it looked like he did his rounds. None of us knew it or we would have stopped him. It was a good job. Don't worry, I'll find another."

I hope I can be like Uncle Al when I grow up. He never complains. I've never seen him without a smile.

CHAPTER 32

Winter Camping

⌒

It's the day after Thanksgiving and I have to talk to Mom and Dad about the camping trip. I got the permission slip last Wednesday from Mr. DeAngelo and I haven't given it to them. Well, I guess this is as good a time as any.

"Ma, Dad, I've got this permission slip from Mr. DeAngelo for camping. Would you sign it, so I can bring it back next Wednesday?"

Mom and Dad take a few minutes and read. Mom's the first to speak. "Out in the cold with that foot!"

I knew it and I say the first thing that comes to my mind: "I can't go without it." It wasn't the right thing to say. It sounded funny in my head.

"Don't you get smart," Mom scolds.

I have to switch here, be more persuasive or beg, but Dad cuts in, "Honey, I'll talk with Mr. DeAngelo and make sure he watches Ricky, so he's not in the cold too long without being near the campfire."

Mom's face relaxes and she says, "Okay, but I don't want him to lose that foot. We'll talk about it after you talk with Mr. DeAngelo." Mom signs the slip; I hope this is over.

Dad's going to the meeting with me tonight. He and Mr. DeAngelo have talked before. It's nice being with Dad. Maybe he'll stay a while tonight. I don't get to see him much. He's either out training at night or fixing people's cars. There's Mr. DeAngelo; Dad's going over to see him. They shake hands. Dad's so much shorter than Mr. DeAngelo.

Some of the older scouts are bigger than Dad. I think when he shakes people's hands, they know he's strong. They don't think of him as being small. I think Dad's the strongest man I know. Here he comes with Mr. DeAngelo.

They walk up to me and Dad says, "Mr. DeAngelo has a battery powered hand warmer. He says you can put it in your boot to keep your foot warm."

A solution, Mom will be happy with that. Less than a month and we'll be camping. I can't wait—I hope it snows.

Today's not a comfortable walking day. It's cold, one of my crutches is pinching me under my arm and I've got another blister on my leg. If my new crutch didn't break yesterday, I wouldn't have to use this old pair. That was the first time I've broken a crutch. I came home from therapy with new crutches, ran into the school to show off my new crutches, and the one on the right broke. That was the end of my day in school. I spent the rest of the day at Aunt Ruth's.

Finally, the day has arrived and we're on our way to camping out for two days. We got a really bad snow storm a couple of days ago. I hope there's a lot of snow at the camp. We're all crowded into Mr. DeAngelo's and the Assistant Scout Master, Mr. Leary's, cars. Not many of us are going, just 11 scouts. Mr. DeAngelo's towing a trailer with all our camping gear. We're on our way. We're telling jokes and singing songs. Larry knows the words to "Sink the Bismarck," "Please Mr. Custer," and "Tell Laura I Love Her." We sing the songs over and over. Mr. DeAngelo likes to change the words to "Please Mr. Custer." I don't think he likes "Tell Laura I Love Her," maybe because it's so sad. The guys think it's funny. I don't think my fellow scouts have much heart.

We've finally arrived after a long ride up into the mountains. We're camping along the edge of the woods with a field in front of us. There's more snow here than at home and it's colder here. At least it's sunny. We've got to put up four tents, collect firewood, build a main fire, and a fire for each tent. Three of us are getting firewood. I'm gonna collect kindling and see if I can find a birch tree; there's oil in the bark. It'll make it easier to start the fires. We've been living in the City so long, I've forgotten what it's like to walk in deep snow on crutches with one leg in a brace that doesn't bend unless I unlock it. I can't do that every time I take a step. Dragging that leg through the snow's a lot of work. Mr. DeAngelo says it's a study in determination. He's right about that. When I take a step with the crutches, they sink in the snow. I have to lift myself and swing both legs forward. At least I can bend the left leg. If my right leg gets stuck, I wrap my left leg behind it and pull it forward. Walking around here, we'll get this snow packed down and it'll be easier.

We've got a lot of big branches, kindling, and I found some birch trees. I've got plenty of bark from some large limbs that fell out of the trees. The branches were sticking up out of the snow. The tents are up. Larry, Billy, Donny and I are in the last tent. Mr. DeAngelo and Mr. Leary are staying in one tent and the other scouts in the other two tents. I've got the main fire started; we'll hang around that one tonight. Next, I've got to build one in front of our tent to cook our supper. We'll have three fires and three scouts cooking for their tent mates. It's already 4 o'clock and getting dark.

I've got the hand warmer in my boot, but it doesn't get hot enough to keep my foot warm. I don't want to say anything to Mr. DeAngelo. I'm not sure what he'd do, like take me home. I can warm my foot by the fire when it gets cold. We're having hot dogs, beans, and brown bread for supper, Dad's favorite meal. At home, we only have it when Mom's sick and Dad has to make supper. It's gonna taste good tonight. Baked beans cooked in a pot and hot dogs over the fire on sticks. Okay, now I've got a problem; I've gotta pee and I don't see any latrines.

I'd better ask. "Mr. DeAngelo, where's the latrine?"

"Oh yeah," Mr. DeAngelo says pensively. "It's supposed to be on the other side of those trees."

Mr. DeAngelo starts for the woods to find the latrine. I follow because I can't wait too much longer. We don't get too far before almost all the scouts follow, I guess everybody had the same idear. The woods are just a small grove of trees and the latrines are outhouses, two of them. Those are gonna be cold when we need to sit. What a blessing to be a boy.

We've finished eating. That had to be one of the best meals I've ever had, not because I'm crazy about hot dogs and beans. I was hungry enough to eat liver and I hate liver. It tastes like hairy meat to me. Mom loves liver. She says there's nothing hairy about it. I'm just glad she doesn't make Donna and me eat it, probably because Dad won't eat it either. We're gonna have s'mores for dessert tonight. We all sit around the main fire; Mr. Leary's gonna tell a ghost story. I've got my right foot as close to the fire as I can without burning it. It feels good. I'm toasting my right foot and my marshmallow. I can't wait to get that marshmallow on the chocolate bar between the graham crackers. I'm drooling; this is gonna be good. We sit at the fire listening to the ghost story, singing songs, and just talking. Mr. DeAngelo's making popcorn for a late night snack as he calls it. It's not even 9 o'clock yet and we're all ready for bed. It feels like it's 11 o'clock.

When we finish the popcorn, Mr. DeAngelo gets up and says, "Okay, scouts, time to hit the sack. Remember, guys, you'll be warmer if you strip to your underwear. Trust me, it's warmer in the sleeping bag in your long underwear." I've heard that before, so I'll take his advice. I've got to take my pants off anyways, so I can take my brace off.

I'm not worried about being warm. I've got a good sleeping bag. It's freezing cold here. Mr. Leary says it's in the single digits. I'm happy he didn't say the number. I think it would make it feel colder. I get up and take a step toward my tent. The bottom of my right boot feels squishy. I lean over, unlock my brace, and lift my lower leg up so I can see the bottom of my right boot. It's bubbled.

Mr. DeAngelo sees it and says, "Looks like you got the bottom of your boot too warm; it's bubbled."

"Yeah, I guess it is," I chuckle. It feels funny walking on it. Can't say my foot's cold.

Our fire's still hot; I'll put some kindling and logs on it. Gonna need some coals in the morning. I take another walk in the woods to relieve myself, no need walking all the way to the outhouse. It's dark out here. Without the flashlight, it's pitch black. There's no moon tonight but plenty of stars. I get back to the tent and get my clothes and brace off. I'm warm as toast in no time. I can't keep the brace in the bag. It's too uncomfortable and I've never been able to sleep with it on. It's gonna be cold in the morning, I'm starting the fire and making coffee. We don't say five words and we're all asleep.

It seems like I've only slept for a few minutes and I'm awake. My head's in the bag. I'm short enough to get all the way in the bag. My feet are up against something hard. What's that? I slide up and stick my head outta the bag. The stars, how come I see stars? Where's the tent? There it is; it's behind me. What? Where am I? I'm outta the tent. The flaps are tied closed. How did I get out here? My feet are against the stones around our fire. The fire has burned down, but the coals have to still be hot; the stones are warm. Thank God the stones are there. Seems I'm trying to burn my foot off, not freeze it.

Now how did I get out here? I don't want to get outta the bag. I can reach the tent; I've got hold of the floor of the tent. Maybe if I hold onto the bag with my left hand I can pull myself back to the tent. The packed down snow's like ice. Our fire's slightly downhill to the tent. I didn't notice we were on a slight hill. I slid outta the tent, I must have. If the guys pulled me out, they'd be laughing and I can tell that they're asleep by the sound of their breathing.

Okay, I'm at the tent, but I can't pull myself into it. Don't tell me I've got to get outta this bag; this is gonna be cold. Okay, I'm under the flap, in the tent, and the bag's in. Oh, I see. There's a tie on the bottom of the flap and another on the tent floor. The floor wraps up when you tie the flap to the floor. Figures, I'm the only one who slid outta the tent. Got to get warm again and get back to sleep.

CHAPTER 33
First Kiss?

~~

It's morning … already. How LONG can I stay in this bag? Not too long, I'm hungry. We've got bacon and eggs, toast, orange juice, and coffee for breakfast. Mr. DeAngelo said he's going to the reservation office at 7 o'clock to get the food he left there. No way to keep it from freezing out here. The water, orange juice, and eggs would've frozen for sure. It's 6:55 on my watch, gotta get up. The coffee pot's got grounds in it, all I need is the water to make coffee. Gotta get the fire going and perk the coffee; it's been a long time since I remember wanting a cup of coffee this bad. I hear Mr. DeAngelo's car starting. He's going to get the food, time to get up.

"Hey, Larry, you awake?" I whisper.

"Yeah," he answers sounding like he's warm and comfortable. "Whaddya want?"

"Nothing," I answer, "just wondered if you're awake."

I unzip the bag and sit up. Oh my goodness, it must be below 0! There are little balls of ice on the inside of the roof of the tent. It's gotta be moisture from our breathing that froze up there last night. If it had warmed up, we would've gotten rained on. My brace—it's so cold even with long underwear. I get my clothes and coat on, untie the tent flaps on my side, and throw some birch bark and kindling on the coals. We Boy Scouts are so prepared. I've got my waterproof match container in my pocket. I take out a wood match and strike it on the side of the container. The match lights and I hold it to the birch bark. The bark catches and in a few minutes I'm putting small branches on the fire.

Got the fire going and the coffee's perking.

"Billy, Donny, you awake?" I ask.

This time, I don't bother to whisper. We're supposed to be done with breakfast and cleaned up by 8:30. No use whispering, they need to get up. I'd think the smell of coffee would get them up. It could be the temperature that's keeping them in their sleeping bags.

"Yeah, I'm awake," Billy and Donny answer in unison

Billy says, "I'll get up when the fire's going."

"Me too," Donny says through a yawn.

Billy and Donny are brothers. They're like Larry, just regular guys. Donny's the oldest, so he knows how to do more like put up the tent, but he doesn't even know how to boil water. They need to work for the cooking merit badge. I'll get it before them at this rate.

"The fire's going and the coffee's ready!"

The main fire is ablaze and the smell of coffee fills our camp area. Before long you can hear the sound of bacon sizzling in the pan. The smell's overwhelming. The taste of hot bacon and eggs cooked over a wood fire on a cold morning is an experience that everyone should have at least once in their life. Even the burnt toast is good. Loading the toast up with fresh cold butter and strawberry jam makes all the difference. We eat until we can't eat another bite. We're hiking to-day; we're gonna need the fuel. Sitting here eating, I realize I haven't thought about Mary Jane or Micky since we left for camp.

I barely see Mary Jane now that we're in junior high and she lives right downstairs! It doesn't matter, I'm going to see her in a few days at my party. I'm turning 12. Just one more year and I'll be a teenager. Things will change then. I'll have a girlfriend by then. All I gotta do is ask Micky. After I ask her, I don't think I'll have to ask anybody ever again. It's either "Angel Baby" or "Cathy's Clown."

We're cleaned up and ready for the hike. We're hiking until lunch and then we're packing up to leave. Here we go. I'm the only one not carrying a knapsack. That would probably be a little too much. We hike about a quarter of a mile in the snow. I'm really feeling this. The others are taking in the scenery, I'm just concentrating on keeping up. All my energy and focus is on the task. I see some of the other guys are starting to slow down. Maybe we'll stop soon.

Mr. DeAngelo and two of the guys are ahead by a tree looking at the ground. I wonder what they're looking at. I see it. They're looking at a knapsack under the tree. We catch up and now we're all just standing here looking at it. There's enough snow for a boy to be attached to the knapsack and be buried by snow. We can only see the back of the knapsack. There could very well be a boy attached to it. I know we've all got the same thought. Is there a dead scout attached to the knapsack? Mr. DeAngelo's just standing there looking. It kind of reminds me of what Mom said the doctor did when he came to our house the day I had polio—he just stood there.

Mr. DeAngelo says with a sound of finality, "Well boys, I guess we've got to find out." He reaches down, takes hold of the knapsack, and pulls. The sack doesn't move at first; it's stuck—chills go through my body. Suddenly the knapsack pulls away from the snow and the straps hang in the air. There's no scout attached. Some scout must've forgotten it while resting against the tree. A sigh of relief moves through the group and we continue on.

I don't know how far we've walked. I've lost track of time and distance. My arms are numb. I don't think I've ever been this tired, at least not my arms. My left leg gets this tired every week at therapy. I've got to stop to see where we are. There's our camp! I don't know how I missed it. We've been walking across open fields of snow for so long, I can't believe I didn't see the camp. Okay, stop thinking, gotta catch up. We finally straggle into camp. Even Mr. DeAngelo looks tired. Mr. Leary's waiting for us. He's made peanut butter and marshmallow sandwiches for us to eat before we break down the camp. We all look like we're too tired to chew. Mr. Leary's put a lot of our gear in the trailer. All we have left to do is take down the tents and clean the area. We spend the better part of two hours preparing to leave.

We're on our way home. No one has much energy left to talk. We were all gung ho when we left home, full of energy. I can't wait to do it again but not tomorrow. I can feel the start of a blister on my leg. I'm taking it easy tomorrow; I'll worry about it then. The best part of camping out is no one worrying about me. Nobody tried to help me. I wonder how other kids on crutches feel about people helping them. That's funny; I've never seen any other kids on crutches except the two at the summer camp. I wonder where all the other kids on crutches are. A lot of other kids had polio.

We're back. Wow, that didn't seem to take as long as the ride up. I think I fell asleep. There's Dad waiting for me.

"Hi, Dad," I yell as I slide outta the car.

"Hi, Son, how was the camping?" Dad says with what appears to be some pride.

Mr. DeAngelo walks over to Dad and says with a smile, "No trouble."

Dad smiles and says, "I didn't think so."

It sounds like code to me. I wonder what they said to each other before we left. Sounds like I passed a test of some kind. Dad brought the car. We only live a block and half from here, but I'm glad I don't have to walk it. Of course, it would burst the blister. I'm finally in the kitchen and Mom and Donna are waiting.

"So, did you have a great time?" Mom asks.

I can see Dad smiling at her and Mom's seeing it too. More signals I guess. Mom's *I wonder how things went* concerned look changes to a smile.

"I had a great time."

"Whew, that smell of smoke. Take those things out to the back porch. I'll hang them on the line to air them out," Mom says to Dad with a look of horror.

"And you," She's looking at me, "time for a bath."

Mom looks happy and shocked by the smell at the same time. She's laughing as she takes my coat out to the back porch to hang it on the line. Donna hasn't said a word other than ugh; she's pinching her nose closed with her fingers. I fill the tub and take off my clothes and brace. I walk on my knees to the tub and lift myself up to an upright position. The tub at the Project was low, but this tub is different. It isn't part of the wall like the one at the Project. This tub looks like furniture in the bathroom. Mom said it's a claw foot tub, it does have what looks like animal feet that the tub stands on. It makes the tub much higher.

I balance myself on my hands, holding onto the edge of the tub. Then I lift my left leg up into the water and steady myself with my left foot against the inside of the tub. It feels so good. I can feel the steam coming off the water. Now I can smell the smoke. It's coming from my clothes on the floor. I think it smells great. It smells like the camp fire. I sit on the edge of the tub, pull my right leg up, and slowly let it down into the water. Again, it feels so good. I feel the blister as I sit on the edge of the tub and slide into the water. It hurts, but camping out with the guys was worth it.

The days have dragged by between Christmas and my birthday party. All I can think about is the games we might play. Larry knows about some games I've never heard of. I hope our moms go downstairs during the party so that we can play them, at least spin the bottle or even post office. Larry's not completely sure how to play post office, but it seems to have something to do with being in a closet with a girl, alone. He thinks you kiss her and see if she pushes you away. If she does, you try to stay in the closet with her as long as you can and make everybody else wonder. If she doesn't, you kiss her as long as she'll let you or until five minutes have passed. A person watching the time knocks on the door after five minutes. I don't think I could just kiss a girl. I would have to ask her first and I know I wouldn't force a girl to stay in the closet. Larry says you talk with her. It doesn't make a lot of sense to me. Maybe Larry's got it wrong?

Now spin the bottle—that's different. Everybody knows how to play spin the bottle. I'm not sure I can say the words spin the bottle in front of Mary Jane. I'm afraid she'll think I want to play, so I can kiss her. She'd never talk to me if she knew what I'm thinking.

The day has finally arrived and everyone who was invited is here. Not a lot of kids—Bob, Larry, Billy, Fred, Mary Jane, Rita, Leota, and Grace. Donna and Cathy are here too. There are cake and presents and stuff for games. There are prizes too. All I need is a bottle for the game I want to play.

I get Larry alone in the kitchen and say, "Hey, would you mention spin the bottle if Mary Jane's mom and my Mom go downstairs and take Donna and Cathy with them?"

"Sure," Larry says. I think he likes Leota.

Who wouldn't like Leota! He probably wants to kiss her. We open presents, eat cake and ice cream, and play pin the tail on the donkey and darts. We start listening to records and there they go; the moms, Donna, and Cathy are going downstairs.

My stomach tightens with excitement, but what's the chance I get Mary Jane or she gets me when we spin the bottle? It's time.

Larry says to me, "Have you got an empty bottle?"

Do we have empty bottles! I told him to say we're gonna play spin the bottle. I jump up and get an empty soda bottle. I'm so excited I can barely get my muscles to work together to walk across the room.

Billy says, "We're playing spin the bottle, right?"

Hearing the words and no objections is too much. I'm almost unable to move. I can't look at Mary Jane. I know I'll give away what I'm thinking. Could this be the chance I've been waiting for, to kiss her? I know she'd want to be my girlfriend after she kisses me. I'm glad I haven't asked Micky yet to be my girlfriend. Larry suddenly becomes the spin the bottle expert. He says he'll explain the rules. After a long detailed explanation, we all sit in a circle and Larry spins the bottle.

It stops and points at Elaine. He can't say no unless the bottle points at a boy or a relative and he doesn't get another spin until it's his turn again. Larry leans across the circle and gives her a quick kiss on the cheek. I can see he's not happy. We're sitting with all the boys on one side of the circle and the girls on the other. Mary Jane's across from me, as far away as you can be in a circle. When I get to spin, the bottle points at Fred. That figures; I lose my chance. Now I realize that my first kiss could be Grace, Elaine, or Rita. Now I'm nervous. What's the chance?

Elaine's next. She gets Grace so now Leota spins. She gets Billy. Billy's tall and cute. Neither of them seems to mind and it's kind of a long kiss and they're touching lips. Larry grabs Billy's belt in the back and pulls just enough to pull Billy back a little. Billy hits Larry's hand and starts to lean forward to kiss Leota again, but she's leaning back onto the floor. Neither Billy nor Larry look happy, but they don't start anything. Next is Elaine. She gets Larry. I can't believe it; what's the chance of that? It's a quick kiss again and now it's Rita's turn. Rita is cute. Maybe it wouldn't be so bad if she got me, but no, the bottle points at Mary Jane, so Rita loses her chance too. Now it's Mary Jane's turn. I'm a wreck, my stomach is in knots. What if? What if by some miracle the bottle points at me. She has to kiss me. She can't say no. It's the rules.

Mary Jane takes the bottle in her hand and spins. The bottle turns and turns for what seems like forever; I can't breathe. Finally, it slows down and stops. The angels, God—somebody's looking out for me; the bottle is pointing at me. I can't move. In what parallel universe could this possibly happen? The bottle stopped and it's pointing at me! Mary Jane looks up at me. There's no expression on her face. Does she want to kiss me? I can't tell. Does the thought of it make her sick? This would be so much easier if I knew. Is she gonna want a long or a short kiss? I guess I'll find out.

She's slowly getting on her knees, she's leaning across the circle, she puts her hands down in front of me. She's so beautiful. I close my eyes and pucker my lips. I can smell her long auburn hair as she leans closer to me. Her hair touches my cheek. I feel like I did in the car with Rita, but this time, I'm not moving. No, it isn't that I won't move; I can't move. I'm paralyzed from the neck down. I want to lean forward and meet her lips, but I'm stuck. I've imagined this moment for weeks, we would move slowly closer and closer, our lips would touch, and Mary Jane would fall in love with me forever. This is it. I feel her breath; I feel the kiss … on the ear piece of my glasses! What?

There's a noise on the stairs. Mom is coming back up. "Mr. Blue" is playing on the Victrola. It could have been "Come Softly to Me." What happened? Where's my kiss—a real kiss—my first kiss?

CHAPTER 34

Going Steady

A new year, the second half of the school year, and we have a new shop, metal shop. Wood shop is over. Mom loves her cutting board. I sanded and worked on it till it was perfect. Now in metal shop, we're learning about measuring with a ruler and a micrometer. The ruler's easy. Dad uses micrometers, but he hasn't taught me how to use one. Now I'm gonna learn. The micrometer measures in thousandths of an inch, which is really confusing to the other guys in the class. The ruler measures in halves, fourths, eighths, sixteenths, and so on. You just keep cutting the inch in equal parts starting with dividing it in half then dividing the halves in half.

Some of the metal rulers here in the shop are in thirty-seconds of an inch. That's the inch divided into thirty-two equal parts. The micrometer divides the inch into 1,000 equal parts. That's much more accurate. The shaft on the micrometer has marks for ten and hundred-thousandths of an inch, and the barrel that you turn to open and close the micrometer has 10 divisions, each one is one thousandth of an inch. Turning the barrel one full turn opens or closes the micrometer 10 thousandths of an inch. It only takes me a few minutes to learn how to read the micrometer; it's so simple. Billy's in my class and he was having lots of trouble. I finally got him to understand it. I liked helping the teacher, I know I'm meant to be a teacher.

Today I've got a crutch tip blow out. The wood bottom of my crutch is coming through the crutch tip. On the wood floor in school it's dangerous, not so bad on the sidewalk. Wood on wood is like walking on ice. I have to keep pulling the crutch tip off a little to keep the wood off the wood floor. I can't take more than 10 steps without having to stop and adjust the crutch tip. By the end of the day, it'll be two steps. Blisters, worn out crutches, and blown out tips sure happen a lot more going to junior high. Must be all the extra walking. Seems like everything's wearing out so quickly. I'm not getting a callus at the top of my leg. I don't think that skin will form a callus.

Last night I dreamed about the building. I wish I knew what the building is and why I dream about it. I've been praying to God for so many years now about getting rid of the dream. I sometimes wonder if He's listening. Mom says God has his own time and sometimes his answer to prayer is *yes* and sometimes *no not yet*. I think there are other answers. I've prayed to be less tired, about the blisters, about being paralyzed, and it seems I get more to pray about. I can't help but laugh when something else happens like when I was getting the stomach aches. Mom says God has a sense of humor. If we're made in His image, I guess He would. Mom also says I have a strange sense of humor. I hope He doesn't have mine or else I'm in trouble.

"Hey, Rick." It's Larry coming up behind me.

"Hi, Larry."

"Hey, what's that clunking?"

"My crutch tip's blown out,"

"Sounds like you're walking on a peg leg," Larry jokes.

"I know," I agree.

"Hey, peg leg," Paul says from behind me.

"Hey, creep," I say turning to swing the blown out crutch his way.

Paul jumps back and bumps into a girl who hits him with her books.

"Thanks," he says to me.

"Hey, not my fault, you knew I wouldn't hit you."

"I'm not taking any chances."

"Hey, you guys still goin to the dance Friday night?" Paul asks.

"Yeah, why?" I ask suspiciously.

"I might want to start going,"

"Well, stay away from Micky," Larry tells Paul.

I flinch. That's just what Paul needs, an opportunity.

"Micky! Micky who?" Paul questions.

I know he's heard her name before, but he's playing stupid. I know he saw me flinch.

"Micky Asher," Larry answers.

About this time I'm ready to hit Larry with my crutch. He seems to have what Paul calls diarrhea of the mouth. Paul would have said it by now, but he's having too good a time at my expense. Got to get Larry moving to class.

"Larry, the bell's gonna ring," I remind him. "You better get to class."

Larry checks his watch and turns to run and Paul yells to him, "What's she look like?"

Larry doesn't answer.

I answer, "Like a girl!" The bell rings as I duck into class.

Today's Friday and Paul hasn't mentioned the dance all week. Maybe he forgot. Well, once homeroom is over, I won't see him all day. We've got different lunches now, so in five minutes I'm safe. Paul's telling me about his brother getting in trouble with the police. If I keep making believe I'm interested, he won't stop talking about his brother until the bell rings and then I'm outta here. There's the bell and he's still talking. We get to the door and Paul's done with his story.

I'm almost free when Paul says, "Hey, Rick."

I turn without a thought and Paul says, "I'll see ya tonight ... maybe."

Darn it, I thought he forgot. He said maybe. I can only hope he doesn't show up. There's one sliver of hope. I think he did that on purpose. If he shows up, he'll be giving me a hard time all night, it will complicate matters with Micky. I can't ask him not to come, I don't want to hurt his feelings if I'm wrong and he really wants to come to dance. Maybe I'm worried about nothing. I usually am.

Larry and I arrive early to the dance. We're all standing outside waiting for the doors to open and no Paul in sight. I doubt he'd arrive early. If he's coming, he'll come late. Finally, the doors are opening. I don't see Micky yet either, but there's Tommy. He never misses a Friday night. They're playing "Dream Lover." I wish Micky were here.

Sometimes I wish I could get her off my mind. No, I mean I wish I could get asking her to go steady off my mind. I have to do it, but I'm so afraid. If she comes tonight, I'm gonna ask her. I can't take this anymore. There she is. Now I have to beat Tommy to her when the next waltz starts.

"Hi, Micky."

"Hi, Rick," Micky says with a smile. Before I can ask, the song changes and it's "All I Have To Do Is Dream."

This couldn't have been better if I had planned it. I put my arm around Micky's neck and we dance slowly. Now's the time.

I stop dancing, lean back, and say, "Will you go steady with me?"

There's a pause, no sound. I'm so scared, what if she says no. Then Micky says a word—just one word, "Yes."

I can't believe it! It's happened the way I imagined—she said yes! My life's complete. To have a girl want to be with me, just me, that's what I've wanted for so long and tonight it finally happened.

CHAPTER 35

Unsteady

~

The song's ended; I give Micky a hug and excuse myself to find Larry. I act cool as I walk up to him.

"Guess who said yes?" I ask Larry.

"Micky?" he says in surprise.

"Yes!" I almost scream.

Larry slaps me on the back and congratulates me. Then Tommy walks up to us.

"What's the big deal?" He asks.

I'm not gonna say anything, but then I don't have to because Larry blurts out, "Rick asked Micky to go steady and she said yes."

A look of complete horror comes over Tommy's face and he runs off to the other side of the gym. He throws himself on the floor and buries his face in his arms. An hour later and he's still there, but Micky's kneeling down talking to him. I imagine she's telling him someday there'll be a girl for him. I've heard that enough. Some guys get the girls and others don't. This is my time. I wish he'd grow up. I do feel bad he's so upset. I know how it feels. The last song, it's "In the Still of the Night."

What a way to end the night. I've gotta dance with Micky, but she's still talking to Tommy.

Should I go ask her to dance? No, I'll wait …What're they gonna do, talk through this whole song? Everybody's in the way, I can't see Micky and Tommy. There she is. She's going over to her friends.

Oh no, the songs ending. I've got to go say goodbye.

"Micky, I'll see you next Friday?" I ask.

"Yes," she says with a smile as she and her friends rush out of the gym. Tommy's headed my way.

I'm floating. I think I'll float from now on. Hey, Paul never showed. This is the best night ever. I wish Micky and her friends weren't in such a hurry.

"Hey Larry, look, Tommy's smiling." That seems strange.

Tommy walks up to Larry and whispers in his ear.

Larry says, "No way."

Tommy glances at me and runs out of the gym.

"No way what?" I ask Larry.

"He said he's going steady with Micky too," Larry says quietly.

I can't talk or move. What's happened? Larry says he thinks Micky felt bad for Tommy, so she said she'd go steady with him too. I don't care, she can't go steady with two guys. I've got to talk with her. Larry and I walk outta the gym in silence.

We walk two blocks and Larry says, "Are you okay?"

I just look at him. No, I'm not okay. My perfect life just ended. How do I fix it? I've got to talk to Micky.

"I'm going to Micky's house tomorrow to talk with her," I say with all the determination I can muster. "I've got to fix this."

"How are you gonna fix it?"

"I've got to tell her it's me or Tommy."

Now I'm mad, but I'm not sure who to be upset with: Tommy or Micky. This is all new to me. Larry doesn't say anything.

We get to my house and Larry says, "See you Monday."

I wave. I'm not sure I can talk without giving away how much I hurt. I slowly climb the stairs to the kitchen.

Mom yells from the living room, "Did you have a good time?"

"Yep."

I can't say any more. I look in the living room. Mom and Dad are cuddling on the couch watching television.

"Good night," I say.

Good night, Son, "Dad answers.

"See you in the morning," Mom says quietly.

They're happy; they've got each other. I'm alone. I sit on my bed and click on the radio, keeping the volume down. I can't believe what's playing, "Maybe" by The Chantels. I can't believe the timing, the words. I've heard them a hundred times. If I pray every night, you'll come back to me; is it possible? What a beautiful song. And maybe . . . I guess I'll know tomorrow.

"Good morning," Mom says as I walk into the kitchen.

"Good morning, Ma."

I'm dressed and ready to go. I've got to come up with someplace I'm going, which will take me long enough that it won't raise suspicion.

"So what are you doing today?" Mom asks before I have much time to think.

"Uh … I'm going to the library," I respond as matter-a-fact as I can.

"That's good," Mom says.

Whew, got past that one. I know where Micky lives, it's past our school near the Our Lady Hospital. She lives at the end of a long street that's just one block after the hospital. It's a long walk, but it's worth it. I'm confident Micky will see this my way. She's just trying to be nice to Tommy. I can understand that. I hate to hurt anyone's feelings too.

"Egg on toast for breakfast this morning then you need to vacuum and straighten out your room before you go out," Mom orders.

I'm so lost in my thoughts, I almost missed it. "Okay, Ma."

I hate cleaning the house, but I know better than to say anything. Mom always acts like she's right on the edge of anger when she cleans the house on Saturday morning. Dad works every Saturday morning, so he misses these special moments. I always feel like I'm walking on egg shells when we're cleaning. It's only like this on Saturday morning. Last night Dad said we're taking a ride later this afternoon, so I better hurry. I know Mom's not gonna let me go any sooner than she has to, so I better get going with the vacuum.

It takes me less than an hour to clean my room and just as I thought, Mom wants me to dust. I get to dust the whole house. Donna's still working on her room. She's got plenty of time, so she's making a project out of it. Almost another hour, it's quarter of ten, and I'm done with the dusting. Mom's vacuuming and I hope she's ready to let me go.

"Ma, can I go now?" I plead.

"Yes," Mom says, "but don't be gone long, remember, we're going out later.

I want to ask how late, but I'm outta the house before Mom can change her mind. It's almost a miracle I'm out. God's with me on this one. Maybe this will have a good ending after all. If Mom knew I'm going to Micky's, she'd never have let me go. On the important scale, going to Micky's would definitely be at the bottom. The library's at the top. God's got to be on my side. I said enough prayers; it's a beautiful warm spring day and a great day for a walk.

CHAPTER 36

The Building

~

That was a long walk. And there's Micky and her friends playing jump rope. I can't wait to talk to her, just a little further. It figures that the last part of this walk is uphill. Micky must live on the longest side street in the City. Tania's headed my way. I wonder why she doesn't wait till I get there.

"Hi, Rick," Tania says.

"Hi, Tania."

Micky and her friends move to the other side of the street. I wonder what's going on, why doesn't Micky come to see me?

"What do you want, Rick?" Tania asks.

"I wanna speak with Micky."

I'm confused; why is Tania asking me these questions? I start to walk past Tania.

"Wait, Rick," Tania says as she steps in front of me.

"Wait for what?"

"I need to talk with you," Tania pleads.

"What about?"

"It's about Micky," she says softly.

This isn't going well. Micky's got her back to me, she's ignoring me.

"What's going on, Tania?" I ask.

Tania looks down at the ground. She looks like she's hurting more than me.

"Micky's dating a boy in high school."

"Since when?" I blurt out.

"Since this morning."

I didn't think the knot in my stomach could get any tighter.

"She just dropped me like that?"

"I guess so."

I just stand there and look at Micky's back. I don't want to talk with Tania anymore. I've never felt so much pain inside and I can see that Tania's in pain too. I don't want to see Tania hurt.

I smile at her and say, "I'll see you at the dance next week."

I turn around before my eyes tear. I'm not gonna cry, but I'm having trouble controlling the tears I feel coming. This is gonna to be a long walk home. I know why she said yes; she didn't want to hurt my feelings. It's the same reason she said yes to Tommy. That's got to be it. That hurts more than anything else. I'm stronger than that ... I'm fine. It's just not my time. I get home and Mom's in the kitchen sweeping the floor.

"What's the matter?" she asks.

What's this? No matter how hard I try, Mom can see when I'm not happy. Seems like I have to smile all the time or I give it away, she knows.

"Nothin, Ma," I say, trying to muster a smile.

"Oh, something's wrong."

"I asked a girl to go steady and she said yes, but then she broke up with me," I tell her, hoping that's the end of it.

"Don't worry, Ricky; God has a girl for you," Mom says. Mom's Saturday morning anger is gone.

"I know, Ma, I know."

I head for my room.

"You just worry about your school work."

I knew that was coming. I'm not worried about schoolwork; I'm worried about ever finding a girl that likes me, just me. I'd like it to happen in my time. I hear Dad coming up the stairs. We'll be going out soon. I hope Mom doesn't say anything to Dad. I think Dad will hurt more than I do. I know Dad doesn't like my friends. He says they could include me more. I wish he'd not let it bother him so much. They're my friends in school. They just like to ride their bikes. At least Dad doesn't say anything to them.

Dad bursts through the door and loudly says, "Is everybody ready to go?"

Donna and I are ready. I'm very ready, I just want to get away.

"Where are we going, Dad?" Donna asks.

"We're going to pick up some money a man owes me for a job I did and then we're going to a new place to eat called McDonalds. We're going to get hamburgs, French fries, and milkshakes," Dad says with excitement.

Dad's excitement is contagious. Even Mom seems excited.

We're finally in the car and we were driving through parts of the City I know, but now we're in an area we've never been. Well, at least I've never been here. The street is a main street. It's so different from the rest of the City. The street is wider and there are big buildings far off the street with big lawns. The buildings aren't as tall as some in the center of the City, but they take up a lot of space on the ground. Mom says they're insurance companies and that one's a high school, Trade High School. And that building … that one's different. The bricks are yellow. That building … it's the building—the building I've been dreaming about! I jump up on my knees and look out the back window to see the building as we pass by.

"Ma," I yell, "what's that building?"

Mom turns around and says, "Oh that, that's the Municipal Hospital."

"The Municipal Hospital?"

"Yes," Mom says, "remember I told you it's where you stayed when you had polio, they have an isolation ward there."

I can't believe it. That's the building in my dream. It does exist and I was there. I slide back down onto the seat. Now I understand,

I bet I saw the front of that building when they brought me to the hospital in an ambulance or when they took me by ambulance to The Weston when I was discharged. That's the building, it does exist. I'm not making it up. Next time I dream about it, I'll know why.

"I dream about that building, Ma."

"You do? How could you, you weren't two years old yet?"

"I know, but I do," I answer as my voice trails off … "I do."

Painting

Another morning and I'm off to school, it's almost the end of the school year. The teachers don't have much for us to do. It's just as well, we're all ready for summer vacation. Just three more days and I don't have to walk to school until September. That kid walking in my direction looks like he's on a collision course with me. Every time I change direction to go around him he changes. He stopped. What's that in his hand? It's a knife and he's looking right at me. What's he crazy? He's just a kid, he looks like he's maybe in fourth grade. He's holding the knife like he's ready to stab me. He is crazy. I'm bigger than him and we're both alone. I guess I better stop and raise my crutch like I'm gonna hit him with it. Haha, look at him run! What a silly kid. I guess he thought I'd be easy prey. That'll teach him.

"Hi, Ma," I yell to Mom as I walk in the door at the end of the school day.

"Hi, Ricky," Mom yells back.

"Guess what happened on the way to school this morning?"

"I don't know, what happened?"

"A boy was going to attack me with a knife in the Park," I answer.

"What?" she yells as she nearly leaps into the kitchen where I'm still standing by the door.

"Who attacked you with a knife?" Mom asks.

Obviously, this is more important to Mom than it is to me.

"It's no big deal, Ma. I scared him off," I say in an attempt to defuse the panic I see in Mom's face.

"Who attacked you?"

Well, I guess that didn't work. I should have kept it to myself.

"Really, Ma, I don't know who he was. He was just some little elementary kid. I raised my crutch and scared him. He ran," I said trying to defuse.

"Was he one of those kids down the street?" Mom demands.

Boy, she's good. I never gave her the slightest hint and she knows.

"Yeah, Ma, but so what—he was just a kid."

"Wait till I tell your father, well, we're definitely moving," Mom says to me with a tone of finality.

At least I think she was talking to me. She said it as she turned and walked out of the room. It sounds like Mom was looking for a good reason to move and I just gave her one. Poor Dad, he's not gonna have a chance tonight. He's gonna be blindsided. I don't dare get in the middle of this one.

Dad's home the same time he's always home. You could set a watch by him. I'm staying in my room. He's walking up the stairs—he's turning the door knob—he steps into the kitchen.

"Guess what happened to our son today?" Mom starts.

It's the same way I started the conversation with Mom, but Mom's going to use it a lot more effectively than I did.

"Did he get hurt?" I hear Dad say softly, obviously unaware of what's coming.

He sounds like me. He hasn't got a chance. I know what's coming next. I'm going to be in the middle of this any time now. Maybe we can move near Bob. That's what I'll do. If I can't stop the move, I'll direct it. Okay, Dad, call me, I'm ready. Mom dumps the whole story on Dad with a tone of horror.

"Son, come here!" Dad says.

I'm already standing by my bedroom door. I step into the kitchen. Mom and Dad look more relaxed than I expected.

"You were attacked today by a boy with a knife?" Dad asks.

"Not really," I answer. "I scared him off."

"That's my boy," Dad says with pride.

Maybe this isn't so bad after all.

"Are we moving?"

Whoops—where did that come from? Donna! I didn't even know she was listening.

"It's okay, Honey," Dad says as he picks her up. "We've been looking at a house in Town."

A house, in Town? When did Mom and Dad talk about moving back to Town? I didn't hear it. No chance to redirect this one. Cindy … I wonder if she still lives in Town?

It sounds like Mom and Dad have picked a house. Mom just said she's happy with the house. If I don't fall asleep too early tonight, maybe I'll hear more about the house.

"It's gonna need a lot of work, but I'm happy we picked that one too." Dad agrees.

"I hope the kids are happy, but having to spend two weeks here in school won't be easy on them."

What's Mom saying; we're not moving until two weeks after school starts?

"Nothin we can do about it," Dad says. "She can't move into her apartment until the 15th, so we can't move in until that weekend."

"It's gonna be a busy weekend. One day to clean and one day to move," Mom says already sounding tired.

"I guess the 18th will be their first day of school in Town; at least they'll like having the park nearby," Dad says sounding assured.

"I've got to paint the front porch before we move," Dad says sounding as tired as Mom. "I guess I'll get started right after work tomorrow"

Dad's painting tomorrow? I'd love to paint. I think I'll ask if he needs help.

"Dad?" I ask.

"Yes, Son?"

"Can I help you paint?"

Dad looks at Mom. She shrugs her shoulders.

"Well, I guess you can," Dad says sounding a little upbeat.

I can't believe it. Dad said yes I can help him paint. We're painting the front porch white. I'm glad the porch is small; this is my first time painting.

I wonder if I'll be less tired going to school in Town. It was hard this year. Walking to school and changing classes. With homework and exercises, I'm bone tired as Mom calls it. I just don't feel like doing my homework. I've got nothing left; at least tomorrow's Saturday. Yeah, clean the house day but ... I get to paint after lunch when Dad gets home.

"Okay, Son, this is your brush and here's how you put the paint on your brush," Dad instructs as he dips the brush in the paint half way up the bristles and wipes the excess off on the rim of the can. "Now you brush the paint on like this making sure you don't drip paint all over. Start here and paint all the uprights in the railing. Don't miss any spots."

I dip the brush in the can, wipe off the excess, and start to paint. It doesn't take me long to realize that painting isn't as easy as it looks. The paint doesn't cover well in one stroke. It takes several and it seems I run out of paint on the brush before I get one side of one upright covered. Maybe asking to paint wasn't the smartest idear.

"Dad, why are we painting the porch when we're moving?"

"Because it needs it and I offered to do it. The Segals have been good to us and I thought it was the least we could do. So … Son, how was school this year?" Dad asks.

"It was okay; junior high's a lot more walking, though. I get pretty tired."

"You'll get tougher, Son. What's this I hear a girl upset you in school?"

"Upset? Oh, you mean Micky, at the dance?" I answer not looking away from my work.

"I guess so …"

I explain how she said yes to go steady with me and then Tommy, and that she said yes to him because he was crying. Then I find out she's going steady with a guy in high school. I didn't mention I walked to her house.

"I guess she didn't understand what going steady means," I say still not looking away from the task. "I think she didn't want to hurt my feelings," I blurt out without thinking.

"Don't worry, Son. God has a special girl for you."

I can hear the hurt in his voice. I can't answer him. The thought of what happened hurts too much. I can feel my chest and throat tighten. Maybe it's hearing how much Dad cares. I think this hurts him more than it hurts me. That upsets me more. I can't cry. Not now. It hurts so much, but I can't give it away … I've got to be tough. If this is a God thing, I hope he answers my prayers soon.

To Be Continued

Contact Information

If you would like to contact me, please email:

Rich@WEIT-LLC.com